Commercial Banking and Regional Development

in the United States, 1950 - 1960

Florida State University Studies

Number Forty-five

Commercial Banking and Regional Development
in the United States, 1950 - 1960

by

George Macesich

THE FLORIDA STATE UNIVERSITY
Tallahassee
1965

First Printing, August 1965

Second Printing, May 1967

HC
107
.A13
M3
1965

Printed and bound in the United States of America
by Rose Printing Company, Inc., Tallahassee, Florida

vi

THE FLORIDA STATE UNIVERSITY

Published under the Auspices
of
THE RESEARCH COUNCIL
The Florida State University

EDITORIAL COMMITTEE

James Walters, *Chairman*

Karl Dittmer   John S. Simmons
Thomas A. Gleeson   Joseph A. White, Jr.

EDITOR
James A. Preu

To
Taja

TABLE OF CONTENTS

TABLE OF CONTENTS (continued)

LIST OF TABLES

TABLES — continued

L I S T   O F   F I G U R E S

PREFACE

Economists writing on economic development have tended to neglect the role of commercial banking in the process. This book attempts to fill part of the gap. It also reflects the special interest in the development of the Southern United States by its emphasis on banking and monetary conditions in this region.

The analyses in the study draws extensively on data for operating ratios of member banks — a hitherto largely untapped source of information on banking conditions. I am grateful to Dr. Charles T. Taylor, Federal Reserve Bank of Atlanta, for first suggesting to me the availability of these data.

My thanks also go to my colleagues Professors Zarko G. Bilbija, Marshall R. Colberg, William P. Dillingham, M. L. Greenhut, William Laird, S. J. Knezevich, Charles Rockwood and Richard Wallace for their valuable comments and suggestions at various stages of the study. I am indebted to the Inter-University Committee for Research on Economic Development of the South for financial assistance which partly made this study possible. I should also like to express my appreciation to Mrs. Genelle P. Jordan and Mrs. Eddine Kessler for typing and proofreading the manuscript and to Mr. Jan Duggar and Miss M. L. White, for research assistance as well as to many of my students in economics 415, "Advanced Money and Banking," Florida State University.

Tallahassee, Florida
1965   George Macesich

CHAPTER 1

HYPOTHESES CONCERNING SOUTHERN DEVELOPMENT

I. Tradition and External Environment

In a thought provoking Presidential Address before the Southern Economic Association William H. Nicholls in 1959 argued that the South has yet to make a choice between tradition and progress.[1] According to his view Southern tradition consists of five key elements all of which have either a pervasive or largely negative effect upon the region's economic growth and progress. First is the dominance of agrarian values; second is the rigidity of the social structure; third is the undemocratic political structure; fourth is the weakness of social responsibility; fifth is the conformity of thought and behavior.

The dominance of agrarian values works against progress because of its bias against business activity. Such values insulated the large planter from the blasts of economic competition. As a consequence, he has been able to maintain through the years the political, social and economic *status quo*. Agragian values also manifest themselves in a "strong love of the land and outdoor life" thereby creating the belief that Southerners are unsuited for the discipline of the factory system. And probably worse still, these values have made a tradition of leisure, discouraging economic enterprise and producing in its wake laziness and lassitude on the part of the general white and Negro populations.

The rigid rural social structure has perpetuated an "aristocratic ideal" but without the acceptance of *nobless oblige*. The South's "undemocratic political structure" has among other things perpetuated "political control by a coalition of economic conservatives and racial extremists." Weakness of social responsibility in Southern tradition takes many

---

[1] William H. Nicholls, "Southern Tradition and Regional Economic Progress," *The Southern Economic Progress*, January 1960, pp. 187-198 and his book *Southern Tradition and Regional Economic Progress* (Chapel Hill: University of North Carolina Press, 1960).

forms. But the most critical, from the point of view economic progress, is the failure to provide adequately for public
education. Finally, the Southern tradition of "conformity
of thought and behavior" has placed into a straight-jacket
the development of intellectual capacity so necessary for
economic progress.

If Professor Nicholls' prognosis of the Southern malaise
is correct the implications for recovery are indeed ominous
He has devoted a considerable amount of time and effort in
determining what it is that ails the South. And he may well
be correct.

On the other hand, it may be that Southerners are no
better, or for that matter no worse, than other Americans.
Such differences as exist I would attribute to the relative ethnic homogeneity in the South and the lack of such homogeneity in other parts of the country, particularly the North. The
gap between the South and other regions of the country became particularly pronounced between 1890 and the outbreak
of the First World War. It was in the years following 1890
that the United States could no longer be considered a special
preserve for General DeGaulle's "Les Anglo-Saxons."

As carriers of diverse cultural heritages the new immigrants served to stimulate culturally, economically, and politically the regions into which they settled and where for the
most part their descendants still live. It is a remarkable fact
of economic development that the inventions and innovations
have more often than not been affected by aliens.

These immigrants did not settle in the South to any extent for many reasons of which economic is only one. For all
practical purposes the South remained for many years ethni-
cally homogenous with its power structure in the hands of
"Les Anglo-Saxons." Given that this group also constituted
the majority of planters, Professor Nicholls' hypothesis may
indeed be useful in gaining some insights into problems of
development.

It seems, however, that all of this is now changing and
particularly since the World War II years. Provincialism and
regionalism no longer appear to be very important even
though policies have a life of their own and continue long
after the conditions that produced them have changed. South-

erners are going North and Northerners South. And who can say, the various regions of the country may even benefit from their respective "aliens."

Some will point to Southern "last stands" and legislation directed against the Negroes as evidence that this is not true. I would suggest, however, that before we wring our hands and raise a hue and cry against "Southerners", it would be well to reflect also on the activities of those elsewhere in the country and their equally fumbling attempts to preserve ethnic homogeneity. No better illustration of such attempts is provided than the post World War I restrictions on immigration from Eastern and Southern Europe and whose spirit still pervades the immigration laws of this country. The fraudulent statistical manipulations used to "prove" the "inferiority" of immigrants from this part of the world and who constituted the bulk of the post-1890 immigration are on par with attempts to "prove" the "inferiority" of the Negroes. If we take the spirit of our immigration laws seriously, Tolstoy, Pushkin, Copernicus, Boskovich, Tesla, Pupin, Michelangelo, Plato, Aristotle, Socrates and even Jesus Christ could not be considered as qualified immigrants. So also it is with the Orientals including Confuscius.

This is a sad commentary indeed. Yet it suggests that the Southern malaise is not Southern *per se*. Its source is to be found in the penchant on the part of some Americans for cultural, political, ethnic and economic homogeneity. Tolerance of differences should be promoted and not stiffled. After all too much heat applied to the "American melting pot" does not necessary result in a better stew.

II. CENTERS AND PERIPHERIES OF ECONOMIC DEVELOPMENT

Consider an hypothesis advanced by T. W. Schultz in his *Economic Organization of Agriculture*. Consisting of three parts, it attempts to explain locational divergencies in economic development.

1. Economic development occurs in a specified locational matrix; there may be more than one such matrix in a particular economy. This means that the process of economic devel-

opment need not occur in the same way, at the same time, or at the same rate in different locations.

2. These locational matrices are primarily industrial-urban rather than rural in composition.

3. The existing economic organization works best at or near the center of a particular matrix of economic development, and it also works best in those parts of agriculture which are favorably situated in relation to such a center. Less satisfactory organization is found in those parts of agriculture which are at the periphery. As Schultz points out, our economic history strongly supports the first two parts of the hypothesis, but there is probably disagreement about the third. He suggests that it is on this proposition that our researchers should concentrate to determine the empirical validity of this part of the hypothesis. While his hypothesis was advanced primarily for agriculture, it may also be significant for the capital funds market, including commercial banking, and, as a consequence, for the economic development of the South.

One implication of the third proposition of Schultz's hypothesis is that interest rates charged by banks in the South will exceed those charged in the more developed areas of the United States. Another implication is that bank rates within the South will be lower in the urban centers than in small cities and rural regions. We should accordingly expect to find significant variation between interest rates charged in centers of economic development and rates charged on the peripheries of such development owing in fact to the greater risk of enterprise on the peripheries.

III.   STAGES OF ECONOMIC DEVELOPMENT

In his studies of economic development Colin Clark has maintained that as a country develops, the proportion of its working population engaged in primary production (agricultural, forestry, and fishing) declines, the proportion in tertiary production (commerce, transport, services) increases, and the proportion engaged in secondary production (manufacturing, mining, building) rises to a maximum and then begins falling. This suggests that a country reaches a stage of maximum industrialization beyond which industry begins to decline relative to tertiary industries.[2]

Clark also argues that diversion of labor from primary industries to the tertiary service industries is both an effect and an indicator of a rising standard of living. According to his argument, low real per capita incomes are associated with a low proportion of the labor force engaged in tertiary industries and a high percentage in primary industries. A high average per capita income compels a large proportion of the labor force to enter tertiary industries. An explanation for such a movement of resources is to be found in the demand side. As income rises the demand for the output of tertiary industry rises and since this output is in the form of services which are not transportable they must be supplied within the country concerned.

Although Clark's hypothesis has been the subject of critique, it may be important for regional development within a country.[3] Such a distribution of occupations may also have important implications for the development of banking. Consider the critique by Bauer and Yamey. They argue that, first, a substantial portion of the output of tertiary industries are not luxuries with a relatively high income elasticity of demand. Indeed, some products of primary and secondary industries are such luxuries. Secondly, in the course of economic development large substitution of capital for labor may occur in the tertiary industries. Thirdly, the concept of income elasticity of demand applied to the entire economy raises serious problems of aggregation rendering doubtful any generalizations about changes in its value in the course of economic development. This is particularly true when relative prices and the distribution of income change in the course of economic development.

Something of Clark's hypothesis seems inferred for the South by Ratchford when he argues that the area is moving

[2] See Colin Clark, *Conditions of Economic Progress* (London: Macmillan, 1940) ; W. S. Woytinsky and E. S. Woytinsky, *World Population and Production* (New York: Twentieth Century Fund, 1953).

[3] P. T. Bauer and B. S. Yamey, "Economic Progress and Occupational Distribution," *Economic Journal*, December 1951, pp. 151-154; G. M. Meier and R. E. Baldwin, *Economic Development* (New York: Wiley and Sons, 1962), Chapters 8-9.

into a more advanced stage of industrialization.[4] Acceptance of ideas and values presumably commonplace in the rest of the United States has been simultaneously a consequence and cause of the region's development. And apparently as their incomes have risen, Southerners have developed a stronger demand for the products of an industrialized and urban society. This is certainly a more optimistic appraisal of Southern capacity and tolerance for change than that expressed by Nicholls.

IV.   THE SOUTH'S "ADVERSE-BUSINESS MIX"

Professor Edgar S. Dunn advances the argument that "the major reason why the South has been the dominant slow-growth region in the nation is because it has been struggling under the handicap of an adverse business-mix."[5] For the two decades in the period 1940-60 the South, according to Dunn, has been plagued by the dominance of such slow growing industries as agriculture. And in so far as the manufacturing industry is concerned the South suffers from specialization in the slow growth sectors of the industry. What competitive gains the South has made have been nullified by large composition losses. For example, Dunn argues that the fabricating on durable goods industries are the rapid growth sectors of manufacturing whereas the non-durable sectors wherein the South specializes are slow growth. The net effect has been composition losses so severe in such states as in the two Carolinas as to create outward shifts in total manufacturing employment in these states.

It is not the purpose of this chapter to argue the pros and cons of Dunn's interesting hypothesis. Suffice it at this point to note that the South may have had little choice in "selecting" industry on the wobbly criterion of "fast growth and slow growth." Most people will, I believe, agree that after

---

[4] B. U. Ratchford, "Patterns of Economic Development," *Southern Economic Journal*, January 1954, p. 224.

[5] Edgar S. Dunn, "Industrial Development in the South." A paper delivered before the Conference on Area Development, Athens, Georgia, January 8, 1962, p. 3. See also his monograph *The Changing Economic Structure of the South and Its Implications for Economic Development* (Gainesville: University of Florida Press, 1962).

all halitosis is better than no breath at all. So too, an adverse business mix may be better than no business at all.

V. THE SOUTH: AN INTEGRAL REGION OF THE UNITED STATES

Another view which is closely associated with regional aspects of the doctrine of comparative advantage argues that the South is an integral part of the United States. There are no frontiers that prevent or restrict the movement of resources among the various regions of the country. Such restrictions and imperfections as may exist in the various product and factor markets in the South are not unique to the region but exist in other parts of the country as well. The lag in Southern development can be attributed to the process wherein the market is slowly but surely grinding out results.

Something of this sort is suggested by Stephen L. McDonald when he argues that the "south's peculiar resources achieved their new relative importance because the nation's technology reached a certain stage and its population a certain size."[6] There is simultaneously a movement of labor out of the South and movement of capital into the region to take advantage of the South's resources. This process is speeded up when national expansion is rapid and conversely.

---

[6] Stephen L. McDonald, "On the South's Recent Economic Development," *Southern Economic Journal*, July 1961, pp. 39-40. See also Charles T. Taylor, "Patterns of Regional Growth in the United States." A paper delivered at the Conference of Area Development, University of Georgia, Athens, Georgia, January 1962.

CHAPTER 2

THE AMERICAN MONETARY MUDDLE:
AN HYPOTHESIS

I. ROLE OF MONETARY FORCES

Hypotheses discussed thus far overlook one important if not primary influence. This is the role that monetary forces played in creating a favorable atmosphere for economic stagnation not only in the South but in other regions of the country as well.

Inherited mistakes are not easily corrected — particularly when such mistakes are deeply rooted in myth and folklore. Nowhere is this better illustrated than in the cases of the specie standard with its fixed exchange rates and the "real-bills" doctrine. Attempts to escape such servitude is in effect the monetary history of the United States. Many of these attempts failed resulting in an even more severe monetary squeeze. For the most part their failure can be attributed to the unfavorable atmosphere generated by defunct monetary ideas. The remainder of this chapter will develop in more detail a number of these points.

II. SEARCH FOR SPECIE SUBSTITUTES: AN EARLY
AMERICAN AVOCATION

Scholars argue that the colonial system established sources of raw materials and markets for the manufactures of the mother country, while gold and silver were to go the other way.[1] The North American colonies, however, were unable to produce any appreciable quantities of precious metals. The little gold and silver that was obtained came from illicit trade with the Spanish colonies and subsequently drained away to England in payment for manufactures. These circumstances placed the North American colonists under great pressure to provide substitutes for metallic money. Tobacco, salt,

---

[1] Gerald T. Dunne, *Monetary Decisions of the Supreme Court* (New Brunswick: Rutgers University Press, 1960) pp. 6ff.

wampum, and many other commodities were used by the
colonists in place of metallic coin. Massachusetts in 1690
passed a law providing for ten-shilling "indented bills" to
pay off the militia. These bills were accepted for the payment
of taxes and provided the first paper money without metallic
backing in the New World.

Other colonies followed this example. The quantity, security, redeemability and legal tender character of the issues
frequently varied even within a single colony. Since many of
the colonies tended to overissue paper money, some scholars
have regarded all colonial paper money issues as the crudest
form of currency experiments. Other scholars, however, dem-
onstrate that some colonies such as Maryland and Pennsylvania successfully maintained the quality of their paper money
issues.[2] In all of these monetary "innovations" Southerners
played an important role. Besides Maryland such other Southern colonies as South Carolina in 1712 established a bank
for the purpose of issuing paper money based on loans pledged
by property. And Virginia in 1730 organized a bank which
issued notes backed by tobacco stored in warehouses. Indeed,
in the colonial period only Georgia lacked a similar organization.

At the outbreak of the Revolutionary War, the Continental Congress was forced by its inability to tax the separate
colonies sufficiently, to print money as the principal means
for financing the war. The issue of paper money by the Continental Congress was legalized in 1777 by the Articles of Con-
federation. Congress used its powers very liberally and de-
nounced anyone who refused to take its continental dollar
"as an enemy of the liberties of the United States." The states
were requested — sometimes with success — to make Federal
paper legal tender. Rather than by direct levies, taxing thus
proceeded by price level increases.

When independence finally came the continental dollar
was paid off in specie at one fortieth of par. This payment
was made "in the face of the twelfth Article of Confedera-

---

[2] Clarence P. Gould, *Money and Transportation in Maryland* (Baltimore:
The Johns Hopkins Press, 1915) and Richard A. Lester, "Currency Issues to
Overcome Depressions in Pennsylvania, 1713 and 1729," *Journal of Political
Economy*, June 1938, pp. 324-375.

tion asserting 'solemn pledge' of 'the United States and the public faith' for payment and satisfaction.[3] The record of the Southern states is about on par with states elsewhere in the country. Thus, for example, "Washington, who had refused compensation for his Revolutionary service, then came home to have his mortgage paid off in Virginia paper worth ten cents on the dollar."[4]

III. The "Real-Bill's" Doctrine: A Criterion for Sound Banking?

A reading of American banking history suggests that banks along the Atlantic seaboard were at the very outset distinctly commercial enterprises. For the most part banking was in the hands of merchants who made loans for short time periods to other merchants. Such loans were considered self-liquidating because they were secured by goods in process of exchange. "Commercial paper" so derived together with loans to government filled the portfolios of early American banks in the principal Eastern financial centers.

The story in Southern states as well as in those Western states along the rapidly developing frontier west of the Alleghanies is very different. One reason for the difference is that economic interests in these areas were primarily agricultural and not commercial. Banking practices considered prudent and useful on the Eastern seaboard received little sympathy from customers whose interests were not served by short term merchandise loans. The demand for credit in the South and West was long-term so that banks in these areas had increasing difficulty in following the mercantile banking tradition. In order to survive these banks were forced to experiment and in effect write their own textbooks. For their efforts the Southerners and Westerners received little else than abuse and criticism from Easterners who, for the most part, were ignorant of economic conditions in the South and West and the very bases on which these criticisms rested.

Critics of such experimental banking drew their support from the intellectually defunct mercantile banking tradition.

---

[3] Dunne, *op. cit.*, p. 9.
[4] *Ibid.*, p. 11.

Their doctrinaire views failed to take into account the two nonsense propositions on which this tradition rested. The first is that if banks restrict themselves to discounting "real bills of exchange" a country's bank money will expand only in proportion to the "needs of trade."[5] Converse circumstances would prevail when trade declines. The second proposition and closely associated with the first, is that a country's currency will have a "desirable elasticity if commercial banks only maintain a reasonably liquid reserve position and operate competitively."

If this so-called "real-bills doctrine" is considered in isolation from any bank reserve limitations, its shortcomings as a criterion of bank performance and a principal of banking regulation are clear-cut. Each commercial bill can be discounted *ad infinitum* during its short life. Furthermore, valuation of the goods in process is arbitrary. The volume of bank credit is thus limited neither by the "intrinsic" value of any one credit grant nor by the number of grants of any one corporation.

IV. CHARACTER OF EARLY AMERICAN BANKING

American banking did not develop, as it is so often asserted, from a position of weakness into a position of strength. Its history is better described as a series of ups and downs. Quantitative data such as are illustrated in Figure 2.1 do not reveal the vast differences in the quality of early banks; qualitative differences in these state chartered institutions, whether privately or publicity owned are perhaps better indicated by the quality of their notes which furnished a principal component of the American money stock. Some public and private banks kept their note issues as "good as specie" by means of complete and immediate redemption in gold and silver while others made redemption a very speculative business indeed. Banks that operated on a shoestring came to be known as "wildcat banks" because of a tendency of their operators to conceal redemption offices in geographically inaccessible locations, e.g., swamps, forests and in the saddle

---

[5] Lloyd W. Mints, *History of Banking Theory* (Chicago: University of Chicago Press, 1945).

Figure 2.1

NUMBER OF BANKS, 1834-63

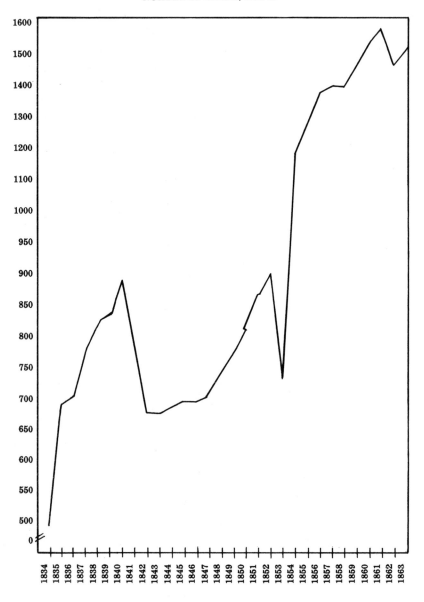

Source: *Historical Statistics of the United States,*

Series X 20-41

bags of fast horses. Banks that "suspended" specie payments did not go into bankruptcy immediately; many states had laws allowing a year's grace to "resume." Furthermore, note holders including other banks were loathe to claim specie when they knew that the banks which were under pressure of redemption might collapse. Bank suspensions tended to spread like an epidemic. The legal expenses of bankruptcy were formidable.

Some idea of the American "monetary muddle" may be had by considering that the notes of hundreds of banks circulated in any community. Their degree of monetary prestige varied. Some were as "good as specie"; some worth half their face value; and some counterfeit. In fact, the difference between a "legitimate" paper issue was one of degree and not of kind. The discount on a particular issue in part expressed the degree of difference as well as the routine cost of redemption in specie of sound notes. Matters were further complicated by the fact that the more dubious an issue of bank notes the more likely the notes would not be loaned out in the vicinity of the issuing bank, but used to purchase merchandise far from home for resale at a profit. If unskilled in exchange, the merchant to whom one of these notes was offered had little choice but to take it upon some terms. In order to determine the validity of the notes and their approximate worth in gold and silver, the merchant turned to his "banknote detector." A Commercial publication developed and used in the pre-National Bank Act era, the detector is mute testimony to the conditions of monetary affairs within the United States. In December 1842, for example, Bicknell's Counterfeit Bank Note Detector, in addition to providing current economic intelligence, reported that notes of some banks in different states were worth fifty cents of specie per paper dollar.[6]

Various legislative measures taken to correct "abuses" in American banking suffered from the defunct ideas of the times. As judged by those espousing the real bills doctrine, Louisiana is a notable example in the pre-Civil War period of a Southern state with a "bound" banking system. The reason for this is not difficult to discover when account is taken of large commercial interests in New Orleans. These interests undoubtedly swamped other economic interests and established by the Louisiana Banking Act of 1842 perhaps the best throught-out banking legislation in the country — albeit in the "correct" mercantile tradition. The Act required Louisiana banks to maintain a specie reserve equal to one-third of liabilities. In true mercantile tradition the other two thirds were to be backed up by non-renewable commercial paper of ninety days or less. In order to provide an incentive for accurate record keeping in banks the Act held directors individually liable for all "illegal" loans unless they could prove having voted against them. The Act attempted to provide for the maintenance of adequate specie reserves in banks by the requirement that each bank pay the specie balances due to other banks every Saturday, or be put into immediate liquidation. Attempts to discourage so-called shoe-string operations rested with the requirement that no bank could pur-

---

[6] Advertisements for the notes of broken banks appeared regularly in the financial sections because these notes could be used as claims against the existing capital of the broken banks. Thus Bicknell continually issued the following form. In 1835 he advertised:

"Broken Bank Notes Wanted"

The subscriber having received an order for the following sum of notes of Broken Banks, will purchase same, in lots, at the following prices:

$5,000	Bank of Maryland	at $.20 on the dollar
4,000	Susquehanna Bridge payable at Md. Savings Inst.	at $.40 on the dollar
1,000	Bank of Alexandria	at $.80 on the dollar
500	Bank of New Brunswick	at $.20 on the dollar
500	Farmer's Bank	at $.30 on the dollar
500	Salisbury Bank	at $.50 on the dollar
250	Comm. Bank Milling	at $.90 on the dollar
250	Westmoreland Bank	at $.75 on the dollar

Robert T. Bicknell
No. 2 Philadelphia Exchange
Bicknell's *Counterfeit Detector,* Vol. III, No. 1, April 1835.

chase its own stock, or lend anyone more than thirty per cent of the market value of the bank's own capital.

Other Southern states also took the lead in "banking reform." Virginia in 1837, for example, enacted the first legislative reserves requirements in the United States by calling for a 20 per cent specie reserve against bank notes, although Congress in 1835 almost passed such a law for the deposit banks of the government's funds. Nine years later Maine in 1846 followed the lead of Virginia and established reserve requirements against notes. And prior to the panic of 1857 only Louisiana and Massachusetts required that banks maintain a reserve against both bank notes and deposits.

Of course, the concept of reserve requirements in American monetary affairs has greatly changed from the original purpose of insuring payment to note holders and depositors. When reserves became legally required, they could not be paid out — a situation analogous to building a fine fire house, placing in it a powerful fire engine, and then locking the fire house and throwing away the key. Reserve requirements are now a control device that limits the expansion of bank credit.

The shaky principles underlying various legislative attempts at banking reform are only partly responsible for the 19th century American muddle registered in history as the "wild-cat" banking era. The operation of the specie standard and capital inflows from abroad before the Civil War were probably the greater generators of this muddle.[7] The United States, as a country on the specie standard during much of the 19th century, like any other participant, will operate under the restrictions imposed by that standard. As a minor country in the 19th century the United States adapts to, rather than creates, the conditions of the specie standard.

Under a specie standard the exchange rates are fixed within specie points, with the result that the internal price level in the United States is at first determined by the external price level. The internal price level must be of a value relative to the external price level such that payments, including capital flows, balance. Consequently, the internal money sup-

---

[7] For a more detailed analysis see George Macesich, "Sources of Monetary Disturbances in the United States, 1834-45," *Journal of Economic History*, September 1960, pp. 407-434.

ply is determined by external conditions, but its composition may be affected by internal monetary circumstances. Nevertheless, a special explanation for domestic disturbances can arise only if internal prices move differently from external prices.

Domestic conditions can affect the internal price level appreciably insofar as they affect the conditions of external balance. For example, suppose internal monetary (bank credit) expansion threatens suspension of specie payments. A price level sufficiently low relative to the external price level that a surplus will arise which finances the capital outflow.

If the country is not on a specie standard, the situation is different. Internal monetary changes affect the price levels and through it exchange rates, so the price level is no longer rigidly linked to price levels abroad.

The primacy of external factors on internal price levels is important because internal monetary disturbances may be simply a manifestation of disturbances more fundamental in nature. Erratic capital inflows and outflows into and out of the United States prior to the Civil War are but cases in point. The increase of capital inflows required an increase in the internal money stock in the United States. The only question was how. An expansion of bank notes issues and deposit credit would not be a reason for an increase in the money supply; it would be only one form of a rise that would have occurred in one way or another. In other words, an internal balance would be consistent with external balance only if the domestic money supply would increase. And, of course, the opposite would occur for periods of world deflation and cessation of capital imports.

Consider, for instance, the sharp price decline in the United States from 1839-43. External prices also declined and the required internal price fall in the United States was further intensified by the cessation of the capital inflow of earlier years and by some repatriation of foreign investment. This contraction had important effects in the banking structure of the United States, namely: the destruction of the Second Bank in 1841, and about a 25 per cent decrease in the number of banks from 1840 to 1843. The collapse of the banking system was one of the forms by which an adjustment, forced by other circumstances, worked itself out. The price decline abroad, cessation of the large capital inflow of earlier years, repudiation of obligations, suspensions of specie payments by some banks, and distrust both at home and abroad of the maintenance of the specie standard by the United States made a sizeable decline in prices the only alternative to the abandonment of the specie standard and depreciation of the dollar relative to other currencies. Given the maintenance of the specie standard, such an adjustment was unavoidable; if it had not occurred partly through the banking collapse, it would have done so in some other way — for example, by an export of specie. Along with the rest of the country such Southern states as Alabama, Mississippi, Florida, Arkansas, Louisiana, Georgia and the Carolinas contributed their share to readjustment by banking collapses and repudiation of both domestic and international debt.

Reactions to these various adjustments took many forms including those already discussed. On the national level, Andrew Jackson's "hard currency" schemes and the Specie Circular of 1836 are perhaps the best illustrations of reaction to adjustments generated by external factors which required an expansion of the money stock in the United States. On the local level, prohibition against banking in many of the Southern and Western states is characteristic of the extreme form reaction took to the necessary contraction in the money stock which was partly manifested in the banking collapse of the late 1830's and early 40's.

V. THE SOUTH'S RETURN TO COLONIAL MONETARY STATUS: THE CIVIL WAR AND ITS AFTERMATH

By their association with the winning side, Western states managed to ease if not escape monetary servitude. For the Southern States it is, however, a different story; through defeat they regressed into colonial monetary status.

At the time of their secession the Conferate States had 189 of the country's 1862 banks and their banking system was about on par with the rest of the country. For various reasons Southern bankers showed remarkable restraint in creat-

ing bank notes and deposits during the war.[8] Undoubtedly
a sizeable portion of the 825 million dollar increase in outstanding Confederate Government Notes occurring between
1860 and 1864 entered the banking system where these notes
added to the South's banking reserve. Yet bank notes and deposits in the same period expanded only by three times.

Eugene Lerner correctly argues that one of the principal reasons for the Southern bankers' restraint is that they
had no central bank to turn to during a crisis.[9] They expected
mass withdrawals whenever Federal troops approached. In
order to protect themselves Southern bankers resorted to
credit restraint and a buildup in their reserves. Some indication of the size of these reserves is provided by Lerner in support of his argument. Thus Georgia banks held 47 per cent
reserves in June 1862, and 69 per cent in June 1863; the Bank
of Fayetteville, North Carolina, held 21 per cent in May 1861
and 46 per cent in November 1863; the Bank of South Carolina held 5 per cent in January 1861 and 30 per cent in October 1863; the Bank of the Valley in Virginia held an average
of 41.2 per cent in 1861, 56.5 per cent in 1862, 57.2 per cent
in 1863, and 66.4 per cent in 1864.

In fact, Lerner estimates that as of January 1864 only
$1.20 of bank money was created per dollar printed by the
government. Northern banks, on the other hand, created $1.49
for every dollar printed during the war by government —
almost 25 per cent more than the Southern states.[10]

Though restraint is indicated on the part of Southern
bankers, the same cannot be said for their government. The
Confederate Government returned readily to the monetary
practices of the American Revolutionary War and taxed via
the printing press by issuing Confederate Notes. Indeed, from
July 1, 1861 to October 1, 1863, 68.6 per cent of all the revenue
entering the Conferate Treasury came from the printing
press.[11] "No one," writes Lerner, "planned to finance the

[8] Eugene M. Lerner, "Inflation in the Confederacy," *Studies in the Quan-tity Theory of Money*, ed. Milton Friedman (Chicago: University of Chicago Press, 1956) pp. 169-170.
[9] Ibid., p. 170.
[10] Milton Friedman, "Prices, Income and Monetary Change in Three War-time Periods," *American Economic Review*, May 1952, p. 635.
[11] Lerner, *op. cit.*, p. 169.

war this way. Because it was so financed, inflation became inevitable."[12]

When the Confederacy's currency reform took hold in May 1864 and stock of money declined, the general level of prices also declined. And significantly the decline in prices occurred in the face of military, political and economic disaster. Unable to collect taxes and sell bonds the Confederate Government turned once again to the printing press with the result that prices once again began to increase and continued until the end of the war.

The large drain of manpower into the army during the first two years of the war caused a "once and for all" drop in the South's real output.[13] Blockade and Union armies further reduced the region's output. By the end of the war the South, for all practical purposes, emerged as an economic wreck.

But if the Confederate Government turned the South in monetary matters back to the Revolutionary War; the Union victory went even further and returned the region to colonial monetary status from which it was not to recover until the 20th century. The National Bank Act of 1863 and the annual 10 per cent tax on the issues of state bank notes were in no small measure responsible for subsequent Southern difficulties.

Two principal objectives were to be served by the passage of the National Bank Act. The primary objective was to enhance the market for Federal Government securities in order to further the financing of the War. Second, the United States was to be provided with a uniform and par value currency. Bank note detectors and state bank notes would henceforth find places only in museums and histories of quaint Americana. The Act had as its theoretical foundation the mercantile philosophy of banking, that is, the "real bills" doctrine. The new institution also had an ancillary effect not foreseen by its sponsors. Reserve requirements on the national level and imposal on a significant fraction of banks provided a means for ultimate control of bank credit. The

---

[12] *Ibid.*, p. 169.
[13] *Ibid.*, p. 175.

Act drew from banking experience, especially that of New York State. It provided that any five people who could raise the necessary capital might start a national bank.

A national bank was authorized to have its own notes printed by the Comptroller of Currency who issued them in return for a deposit of government bonds with the Secretary of the Treasury. Banks also were required to deposit with the Secretary an amount of government bonds equal to one-third of their capital stocks. If more notes were desired for circulation, they could be issued provided the bank deposited an additional amount of government bonds, and that such an issue did not increase the bank's note circulation beyond its paid-in capital stock. Total notes authorized were $300 million. These were apportioned regionally, and were expected to fill the vacuum left by the anticipated retirement of state and United States notes.

Unfortunately for the South and its economic future the apportionment of notes did not include the South because of the War. When the War ended, all of the notes had been apportioned. A substitute for these notes was effectively destroyed when in 1865 Congress levied an annual tax of 10 per cent on the outstanding note circulation of state banks. This was a singular disaster for a people that attached such importance to having a currency, even a depreciating one as the Confederate dollar, that they were willing to pay the great amount of resources for it. So great was the price in fact that it enabled the Confederate Government to finance almost 70 per cent of the war effort by currency issues. The resulting monetary squeeze facilitated the economic stagnation that characterized much of the South in the post-Civil War period. It is little wonder that the South, as the early American colonies, became fertile ground for all sorts of "cheap money" ideas.

Unfortunately, we lack a definitive study of how in fact the circulating media of the United States flowed into the South following the War. Theoretically at least, we should expect to observe that the South generated a favorable balance of trade with the remainder of the country and/or received an inflow of such currency from capital imports into the region. In any event a principal generating industry for a favorable balance of trade was undoubtedly that for which the region had a comparative advantage, namely, agriculture. Various discriminatory devices such as unfavorable railroad rates and basing point systems erected largely by Northern economic interests compounded the war devastation and probably worked against development in the South of a broader industrial base. The net effect was that the South entered the 20th century in possession largely of a declining industry which further intensified and complicated the region's economic, political and social problems.

VI. THE FEDERAL RESERVE ERA

The institution developed to meet the various shortcomings of the National Bank Act was the Federal Reserve System. Member banks of the System could obtain extensive amounts of Reserve Bank credit under specified constraints. First, in true "real bills" tradition, the commercial paper they presented for discount or rediscount had to be short-term, self-liquidating, and for goods "actually" in the process of being readied for sale. Second, the rate of discount for Reserve Bank credit was usually somewhat higher than prevailing market rates for the same paper. Third, true to the specie standard, the Reserve Banks themselves ultimately faced minimal gold reserve requirements.

The Federal Reserve System's operations attempted to provide some solutions to banking difficulties but did not furnish all the answers. The desperate economic situation in such agriculture regions as the South and the West were only intensified. Table 2.1 indicates that the period 1921-30 bank failures in the United States reached proportions almost unmatched in banking history. Most of the banks that failed were not members of the System, and were primarily located in such agricultural areas as the South and West that were in the throes of severe economic distress. Efforts by these small institutions to aid agriculture threw them into financial difficulties, but no relief was afforded by the Federal Reserve System. Indeed the System managed to aggravate the situation by upholding the "mercantile banking tradition" and by insisting that commercial paper eligible for discount at Re-

Table 2.1

BANK SUSPENSIONS—NUMBER AND DEPOSITS OF SUSPENDED BANKS: 1919-1933

Year	Number of Suspensions		State Commercial			Federal Reserve System	
	Total	National	Incorporated	Private (Unincorporated)	Mutual Savings	Member	Non-member
1919	63	8	59	1	1	—	—
1920	168	7	136	24	1	—	—
1921	505	52	409	44	—	71	434
1922	367	49	294	23	1	62	305
1923	646	90	533	23	—	122	524
1924	775	122	616	37	—	160	615
1925	618	118	461	39	—	146	472
1926	976	123	801	52	—	158	818
1927	669	91	545	33	—	122	547
1928	499	57	422	19	—	73	426
1929	659	64	564	31	1	81	578
1930	1,352	161	1,131	58	—	188	1,164
1931	2,294	409	1,804	80	2	516	1,778
1932	1,456	276	1,140	37	1	331	1,125
1933	4,004	1,101	2,790	109	3	1,275	2,729

Source: *Historical Statistics*, Department of Commerce, p. 636.

serve Banks be backed almost exclusively by merchandise. Just as in the pre-1914 period, sound banks were forced to close their doors when a run started because they could not rediscount the paper in their possession. In Florida, for example, more banks failed from 1921 to 1933 than were in existence in 1921. Once again the South's monetary belt was tightened.

The Banking Act of 1935 partially cleared the intellectual air of such defunct ideas as that Reserve Banks extend credit to banks only on self-liquidating paper. Such collateral as various forms of Government obligations were thereafter considered as eligible. These obligations could in no way be assumed to vary directly with the volume of business activity. And indeed any asset now acceptable to the Federal Reserve authorities could be pledged for credit advances. Long overdue repudiation of long accepted ideas by the Federal Reserve authorities gradually filtered down to the more "conscious banker" with the effect that the South, long an exponent of "easy money," had the satisfaction of being able to loosen its monetary belt.

It was not until the Second World War, however, that the South received a wholesale infusion of necessary resources for an escape from economic stagnation. Attracted in part by a favorable climate for military operations, defense installations and industries served to create a basis for building in the South a broader economic base.

VII. CONCLUSION

An economist once said that in the long run it is ideas and not vested interests that win. The consequences that largely bankrupt ideas can bring is perhaps best illustrated in the South. The monetary straight jacket that such ideas as the "real bills" doctrine and specie standard with its fixed exchange rates imposed on this region of the country has contributed in no small measure to the South's past economic social and political stagnation. This would appear to be particularly true up to at least the 1930's when the shackles of mercantile banking tradition were loosened, but not removed, from the Federal Reserve. Liberalization of criteria for judging so-called "sound banking" filtered down through member banks increasing their effectiveness to contribute more positively to the country's, including the South's, economic development. These changes, in a sense, have vindicated the South's long struggle for monetary and banking parity with the rest of the country.

Yet monetary parity by itself was insufficient to repair the economic, social and political damages that the Southerners suffered over the years. The vast infusion of resources into the region during and after World War II laid the foundation for further economic progress. But with progress there also come changes in a region's *status quo*. We are indeed witnessing the emergence of a "New South." The current ferment and change in the South owes much to its economic prosperity.[14] It is indeed mute testimony on the inertia that propels "counterfeit Southerners" in their inability to come to terms with the implication of the region's new found prosperity.

---

[14] Such social peculiarities as "racial discrimination" argued by some as an integral part of so-called "Southern tradition" may very well be a manifestation of the region's past economic stagnation. Inadequate economic opportunities caused in large measure by defunct monetary ideas originating elsewhere than in the South combined to restrict the advancement of both the Southern white and Negro. What few opportunities existed were divided among the whites and easily rationalized on the supposed inferiority of the Negro. Even a nodding acquaintance with the hiring and firing practices in "enlightened" northern industrial centers suggests that the Negro is usually the last hired and the first laid off when a slack in economic activity occurs. And the practices of various craft unions on racial matters are too well known to merit comment here.

CHAPTER 3

FEDERAL RESERVE DISTRICTS AND REGIONAL DEVELOPMENT

I. REGIONAL AND NATIONAL ASPECTS OF THE FEDERAL RESERVE ACT OF 1913

The establishment of twelve Federal Reserve Districts in the United States is the consequence of both political and economic forces. These forces are deeply imbedded in America's financial history and go back at least to the rise and fall of the first two United States Banks (1791-1811 and 1816-1836). The heat generated by the controversies over the activities of these two institutions and their branches was sufficiently great to be felt even in the 20th century attempts at national banking reform. They are but manifestations of attempts to loosen the shackles of monetary servitude imposed by defunct ideas.

Attempts to clear the American banking and monetary muddle at the turn of the 20th Century led to the creation by the Aldrich-Vreeland Act of 1908 of the National Monetary Commission. Extensive studies of banking practices before 1910 were made by the Monetary Commission's staff. But the Commission did not limit itself only to studies. It also prepared and recommended a banking reform measure known as the Aldrich Bill. The bill called for the formation of a National Reserve Association to be capitalized at $100 million. The Association was to have its central office in Washington and fifteen branches throughout the country and it was to be owned by the member banks. For all practical purposes it was a central bank with power to rediscount paper for its members, hold deposited reserves without interest, and deal in the open market in United States bonds. Moreover, it might also issue asset currency, provided a 50 per cent cash reserve was maintained.

Unfortunately for its supporters, the Aldrich-Bill rekindled old passions to the extent that it became a political issue during the presidential campaign of 1912. The Democratic Party stood opposed to the establishment of a central bank as outlined in the Aldrich Bill. Its political platform of that year called instead for a systematic revision of banking laws and protection from the "Money Trust" composed largely of Eastern financial interest. These charges are reminiscent of those levelled at the first two Banks of the United States and which contributed to their downfall.

The Democratic Party's victory in the presidential campaign meant the end of the Aldrich Bill. In its place Congress passed the Federal Reserve Act of 1913. It was, in effect, a compromise between proposals to set up massive central banks and no central bank at all. The Act provided for the establishment of a regional system of not less than eight nor more than twelve reserve banks. Thus the fear that the new system would be dominated by the "Money Trust" was somewhat allayed. The Act provided for federal government supervision of the twelve regional banks actually established but with capital and deposits supplied by member banks.

The twelve Federal Reserve Districts and Banks are presented in Figure 3.1. Such a division is usually justified by an appeal to the economic argument that the country is too large and the activities of the different sections too diverse to encompass the entire country in a single region. Sections of the country with similar economic interests formed into single Federal Reserve Districts facilitate bank servicing of the region's economy. Politically, the division is justified by an appeal to democratic ideals. A single region and a single large central bank, so the argument goes, is contrary to the Democratic ideals dominant in the United States since the overthrow of the first two banks of the United States.

The concept of federal monetary authority has advanced since 1913. And reorganization of the Federal Reserve System which occurred since the 1930's is but a case in point. Powers of the central authority have increased. This development is not without mixed blessings. That the central authorities of the System are by no means divorced of such defunct monetary ideas is suggested by various manifestations of the "real bills" doctrines e.g., qualitative credit controls, and the specie standard e.g., fixed exchange rates.

Figure 3.1
THE FEDERAL RESERVE SYSTEM
Boundaries of Federal Reserve Districts and Their Branch
Territories

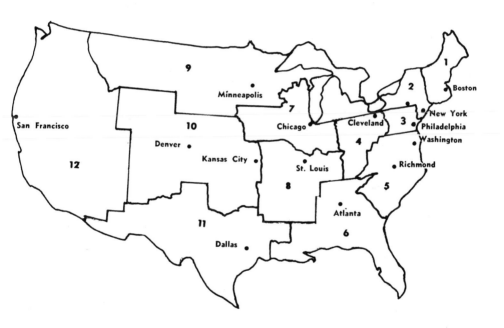

Source: *Federal Reserve Bulletin*

The centralized nature of the System is provided by the example of the ownership of the Federal Reserve Banks. The Federal Government is the "owner" of the Federal Reserve banks and in effect the System. A claim to regional or decentralized nature of the System cannot be achieved by the line of argument that member banks "own" the System. The idea, popular with some people, that it is otherwise is a misconception derived from the fact that the law requires member banks to own "stock" in Federal Reserve Banks.

According to Congressman Patman it is not a stock and it lacks many of the characteristics normally attributed to a bond. Thus, he states:

> ". . . The law makes it abundantly clear . . . that this so-called stock is not ownership stock and carries none of the rights and privileges of stock. This 'stock' cannot be sold, it cannot be voted, it cannot pay dividends, it does not entitle the stockholders to inspect the books, and it does not entitle the stockholders to a share in the assets. Further the law plainly states that even if the Federal Reserve System were liquidated, the so-called stock would have no claim on the assets of the System, except to the extent of the principal actually paid in . . ."[1]

Additional light is shed on this subject in recent congressional hearings. Mr. Patman asked Chairman Martin of the Federal Reserve Board whether member banks have any proprietary interest in the Federal Reserve System. And the following exchange occurred:

> The Chairman: (Mr. Patman) . . . (the proposition) is that the banks own the Federal Reserve Banking System, and it is run by banks, it is operated for their benefit. That is a fallacy, is it not?
>
> Mr. Martin: That is a fallacy.
>
> The Chairman: That stock, or that word "stock" is a misnomer, is it not?
>
> Mr. Martin: If you are talking about stock in terms of proprietorship, ownership — yes.
>
> The Chairman: Well, of course, that is what stock is; yes. Normally that is what stock is; when you say

---

[1] *Congressional Record*, June 2, 1959, p. 8677.

"stock," you mean a proprietary interest of some kind, do you not?

Mr. Martin: You and I are in agreement that it is not proprietary interest.

. . . .

The Chairman: Yes. Therefore the statement that the banks own the Federal Reserve System is not a correct statement, is it?

Mr. Martin: The banks do not own the Federal Reserve System . . ."[2]

Instead of stock ownership what really exists is a sort of forced contract under which a 6 per cent rate of return is paid to member banks to participate in the public enterprise of money creation under rules imposed by the Federal Government. Although Federal Reserve stock is riskless and the 6 per cent of return is generous, it is not an arrangement for the cooperation of equals but the indulgence of a superior — namely, the Federal Government.[3]

II. DISTRICT PER-CAPITA INCOMES. 1950-60.

Economic progress since the passage of the Federal Reserve Act in 1913 may have reduced but it has not eliminated regional differences. The extent of existing regional differences is suggested by per capita personal incomes. Table 3.1 presents the evidence on per capita personal incomes in the twelve Federal Reserve Districts for the period 1950-60. The evidence suggests that during this period personal per capita income in every Federal Reserve District increased. The Districts registering the highest percentage increase between 1950 and 1960 are the 5th (Richmond) by approximately 51%, 8th (St. Louis) by approximately 58%, and the 6th (Atlanta) by approximately 60%. The District registering the lowest percentage increase during this same period is the 1st (Boston) by approximately 41%. The remaining

---

[2] *Ibid.,* p. 8678.
[3] For an analysis of the period preceding and following the establishment of the Federal Reserve System see Milton Friedman and Anna Jacobson Schwartz, *A Monetary History of the United States 1867-1960* (New York: National Bureau of Economic Research, 1963).

Table 3.1

Per Capita Personal Income (1950-60) by Federal Reserve District
(in dollars)

Federal (1) Reserve Districts	1950	1951	1952	1953	1954	1955	1956	1957	1958	1959	1960
1	1629	1823	1908	1958	1938	2076	2214	2298	2302	2388	2471
2	1859	2001	2088	2164	2175	2279	2422	2540	2546	2680	2756
3	1583	1751	1814	1921	1834	1942	2098	2177	2159	2228	2294
4	1614	1870	1958	2032	1924	2061	2183	2253	2159	2283	2339
5	1212	1355	1428	1450	1441	1517	1613	1656	1692	1777	1844
6	1006	1104	1171	1230	1236	1329	1410	1465	1505	1586	1619
7	1653	1841	1909	2015	1959	2055	2164	2224	2187	2294	2349
8	1144	1274	1361	1413	1411	1491	1583	1620	1683	1781	1813
9	1381	1524	1516	1576	1576	1632	1694	1793	1890	1864	1986
10	1347	1505	1630	1609	1627	1642	1709	1822	1942	1981	2078
11	1325	1439	1508	1533	1568	1627	1714	1798	1833	1899	1914
12	1727	1917	2010	2037	2025	2136	2254	2320	2355	2484	2556

¹ States included in Federal Reserve Districts: (1) Maine, N.H., Vt., Mass., Conn.; (2) N.Y., N.J.; (3) Penn., Del.; (4) Ohio; (5) Va., W.Va., Md., N.C., S.C., D.C.; (6) La., Miss., Ala., Tenn., Ga., Fla.; (7) Ill., Ind., Mich., Iowa, Wis.; (8) Mo., Ky., Ark.; (9) Minn., Mont., N.D., S.D.; (10) Kans., Colo., Nebr., Wyo., Okla.; (11) Texas, N. Mex.; (12) Calif., Oregon, Wash., Ariz., Utah, Nev., Idaho. Alaska and Hawaii are members of the 12th but have not been included.

Sources:
(1) Income figures taken from: The 1961 "Statistical Abstract of the U.S.", p. 10.
(2) "Personal Income by States Since 1929", Department of Commerce Publication, 1955, p. 141.
(3) The "Survey of Current Business", Aug. 1961, p. 13.

eight Districts range from approximately a 43% increase (7th District Chicago, 9th District Minneapolis, and 10th District Kansas City) to 47% increase (12th District San Francisco). This is also a period in which the American economy has experienced prosperous times.

Although the effect of these increases has been to reduce District dispersion of per capita personal incomes, the relative per capita income positions of the several Districts has changed little in the period 1950-60.

An examination of the evidence presented in Table 3.2 indicates that per capita personal incomes in the Districts as a percentage of the average per capita personal incomes by year of the twelve Federal Reserve Districts has not changed the position of Districts which in 1950 were at the lowest and highest ends of the scale. Thus, the 5th, 8th and 6th Districts occupied the lowest positions tenth, eleventh and twelfth respectively, in 1950 and in 1960. The 2nd and 12th Districts remained at the highest end of the scale occupying the first and second positions respectively. For the same period four districts changed positions. The 1st District moved up from fourth place to third place with the 7th District falling to fourth place. Two other Districts, 9 and 10, reversed positions with District 10 occupying seventh place in 1960 and District 9 eighth place.

Table 3.2

Per Capita Personal Income by District as of % of the
average Per Capita Income by Year of the 12 F/R Districts

F/R Dis.	1950	1951	1952	1953	1954	1955	1956	1957	1958	1959	1960
1	111.8	111.	112.8	112.2	112.3	114.3	115.3	115.1	114.0	113.6	114.0
2	127.6	121.9	123.5	124.	126.	125.6	126.1	127.2	126.0	127.4	127.1
3	108.6	106.6	107.3	110.	106.3	107.	109.2	109.1	106.9	105.9	105.8
4	110.8	113.9	115.8	116.5	111.5	113.6	113.6	112.9	106.9	108.6	107.9
5	83.2	82.5	84.4	83.1	83.5	83.6	84.	83.	83.8	84.5	85.1
6	69.	67.2	69.2	70.5	71.6	73.2	73.4	73.4	74.5	75.4	74.7
7	113.4	112.1	112.9	115.5	113.5	113.2	112.6	111.4	108.3	109.1	108.3
8	78.5	77.6	80.5	81.	81.7	82.1	82.4	81.2	83.3	84.7	83.6
9	94.8	92.8	89.6	90.3	91.3	89.9	88.2	89.8	93.6	88.6	91.6
10	92.4	91.7	96.4	92.2	94.3	90.5	89.	91.3	96.	94.2	95.8
11	90.9	87.6	89.2	87.9	90.8	89.6	89.2	90.1	90.7	90.3	88.3
12	118.5	116.6	118.6	116.5	117.	117.2	116.9	115.6	116.0	117.6	117.6

From evidence presented in Table 3.3 on the percent of urban population by District, it appears that Districts with the lowest per capita personal incomes also tend to be the least urbanized. Contrariwise, the Districts with the highest per capita incomes tend to be the most urbanized. All Districts registered an increase in urban population in the period between 1950 and 1960. But, as in the case of incomes, the relative positions of the several Districts has not changed much. The 5th and 6th Districts are again at the lower end of the scale while the 2nd and 12th Districts are on the upper end.

Table 3.3

Urban Population as % of Total Population

Districts	1950	1960
1	76.2	76.4
2	85.8	86.2
3	70.3	71.3
4	70.2	73.4
5	46.7	52.4
6	47.3	58.5
7	67.2	71.0
8	47.1	54.6
9	46.7	54.6
10	52.7	63.0
11	62.0	74.0
12	72.4	80.0

Urban population information taken from the 1961 "Statistical Abstract of the U.S.", p. 22. The urban %'s are based on the urban definition adopted in 1950. See Table 3.1 for breakdown of F/R District by State.

III. INCOME SOURCES IN FEDERAL RESERVE DISTRICTS

Table 3.4 summarizes data on the sources of District personal incomes for 1950 and 1960. The evidence suggests that there has been a decline in all Districts in the percentage of

Table 3.4

Sources of Income Received by Persons for Participation in Current Production by Industry & Federal Reserve District

Income (in Millions of $ and as % of District Total by Year for 1950 and 1960)

Federal Reserve Districts	1		2		3		4		5		6	
	$	%	$	%	$	%	$	%	$	%	$	%
Industry Division												
1950												
Farms	341	3.3	563	1.9	380	2.8	468	4.4	1314	9.0	1908	13.8
Mining	19	.2	66	.2	649	4.8	109	1.0	562	3.9	271	2.0
Construction	635	6.1	1529	5.2	745	5.5	563	5.3	1404	9.6	912	6.6
Manufacturing	4775	46.1	9588	32.6	5237	38.5	4502	42.2	3472	23.9	2867	20.7
Wholesale & Retail Trade	2294	22.1	6721	22.9	2547	18.7	2053	17.2	2592	17.8	3026	21.9
Finance, Insurance & Real Estate	521	5.0	1755	6.	432	3.2	309	2.9	423	2.9	500	3.6
Transportation, Communication & Pub. Ut.	754	7.3	2481	8.4	1245	9.2	881	8.3	1113	7.6	1167	8.4
Government	1030	9.9	2566	8.7	988	7.3	782	7.3	2124	14.6	1465	10.6
Services & Other	1403	13.5	4124	14.0	1363	10.0	1001	9.4	1550	10.6	1718	12.4
1960												
Farms	305	1.5	512	1.0	354	1.7	417	2.2	1322	5.4	1824	6.8
Mining	30	.1	97	.2	368	1.7	133	.7	473	1.9	497	1.8
Construction	1181	5.9	2819	5.6	1173	5.5	1056	5.6	1535	6.3	2072	7.7
Manufacturing	7627	37.9	15549	30.8	8537	39.8	7920	42.3	6258	25.7	5868	21.8
Wholesale & Retail Trade	3634	18.1	10674	21.1	3667	17.1	3293	17.6	4351	17.9	5724	21.2
Finance, Insurance & Real Estate	1129	5.6	3438	6.8	880	4.1	729	3.9	1022	4.2	1486	5.5
Transportation, Communication & Pub. Ut.	1201	6.0	4049	8.0	1768	8.2	1428	7.6	1836	7.5	2095	7.8
Government	2095	10.4	5376	10.6	2040	9.5	1745	9.3	4465	18.4	3693	13.7
Services & Other	2916	14.5	8030	15.9	2648	12.4	2021	10.8	3061	12.6	3681	13.7

Federal Reserve Districts

Industry Division	7 $	7 %	8 $	8 %	9 $	9 %	10 $	10 %	11 $	11 %	12 $	12 %
1950												
Farms	3209	9.2	1321	16.3	1400	25.2	1631	21.5	1311	14.9	2007	8.9
Mining	355	1.0	256	3.2	114	2.1	321	4.2	540	6.2	305	1.4
Construction	1766	5.1	452	5.6	353	6.4	500	6.6	697	7.9	1742	7.7
Manufacturing	13141	37.7	1796	22.1	796	14.3	925	12.2	1235	14.1	4536	20.1
Wholesale & Retail Trade	6848	19.7	1743	21.5	1213	21.8	1656	21.9	2005	22.8	5228	23.1
Finance, Insurance & Real Estate	1101	3.2	268	3.3	167	3.0	253	3.3	317	3.6	985	4.4
Transportation, Communication & Pub. Ut.	2674	7.7	798	9.8	496	8.9	748	9.9	830	9.5	1980	8.8
Government	2456	7.1	642	7.9	501	9.0	779	10.2	839	9.6	2750	12.2
Services & Others	3278	9.4	835	10.3	522	9.4	763	10.1	1013	11.5	3062	13.6
1960												
Farms	2505	4.4	1181	8.9	1282	14.8	1509	11.6	1233	7.7	2406	5.0
Mining	386	.7	244	1.9	187	2.2	527	4.1	919	5.7	478	1.0
Construction	3452	6.1	869	6.6	708	8.1	1085	8.4	1165	7.3	3749	7.8
Manufacturing	21428	38.7	3438	26.1	1498	17.2	1971	15.2	2787	17.4	11575	24.2
Wholesale & Retail Trade	10612	18.7	2622	19.9	1782	20.5	2702	20.8	3444	21.5	9564	20.0
Finance, Insurance & Real Estate	2406	4.2	594	4.5	400	4.6	613	4.7	839	5.2	2654	5.5
Transportation, Communication & Pub. Ut.	4158	7.3	1264	9.6	785	9.0	1187	9.1	1449	9.1	3518	7.3
Government	5387	9.5	1350	10.2	1049	12.1	1778	13.7	2032	12.7	6798	14.2
Services & Other	6478	11.4	1612	12.2	1000	11.5	1615	12.4	2124	13.3	7171	15.0

Sources:

Farm income includes net income of farm properties, farm wages and farm "other" labor income.

Government does not include payments to military personnel.

1950 years figures taken from: "Personal Income by States since 1929," a Department of Commerce Publication, published 1955 as a supplement to the "Survey of Current Business".

1960 figures taken from "The Survey of Current Business" August 1961 issue, page 19.

total income received from farms. The same is also true for the mining industry. Percentage of total income received from manufacturing, on the other hand, has increased in the 1st and 2nd Districts where a decline has occurred.

In the case of the several industries presented in Table 3.4 a general and in some Districts a rather sharp increase, has occurred in the percentage of total District personal income derived from these activities. All Districts have also registered an increase in the percentage of income earned in the government sector. Construction, wholesale and retail, finance and transportation industries have a mixed performance rising slightly in some Districts and declining in others.

Except in Districts 9, 10 and 11, the manufacturing industry accounts for over 20 per cent of the personal incomes in the other Districts. There is, of course, a considerable range. District 6 is on the lower end of the range with manufacturing accounting for slightly over 20 per cent in both 1950 and 1960 and District 4 is on the upper end with manufacturing accounting for over 42 per cent of personal incomes.

Wholesale and retailing is another important industry in all Districts and accounts for about 17 to 22 per cent of personal incomes. Service industries and government are the other two most important industries in terms of percentage of personal incomes derived from such activities in all Districts. Transportation and related industries, construction and finance are furthest down the list of importance in all Districts. Farm activity has slipped considerably between 1950 and 1960. Even in Districts 9, 10 and 11, it has fallen behind the contribution of manufacturing. In fact, in these three Districts by 1960, income derived from government approaches (District 9) or exceeds (Districts 10 and 11) that derived from farming.

Thus, a dominant share of personal incomes in all Districts originate in manufacturing, wholesale and retailing, services and government. On this score the Districts tend to be similar. This does not mean that differences do not exist nor that such differences are not important. Yet, a visible drifting toward each other in the past decade has occurred as a result of economic change and progress.

IV. THE SOUTH : A SPECIAL PROLBEM ?

Unless otherwise noted I shall define as the "South" the 5th and 6th Federal Reserve Districts since they contain the bulk of the territory in the United States which once constituted the Confederacy.

To judge from the evidence summarized in this chapter the South does indeed constitute the least economically advanced region of the country. Although percentage rises in its per capita personal incomes outpaced other areas of the country, the region has not changed its relative position in a decade.

In terms of percentage contribution to personal per capita income by the several industries, the South tends to lead the nation in the percentage of revenue derived from government. Even the percentage of incomes derived from farms is only in fifth place compared to other regions. In manufacturing it is also on the lower end of the scale.

But the South in its relative economic backwardness is not unique. In many respects it is similar to the 8th, 10th and 11th Federal Reserve Districts. These Districts are also on the lower end of the per capita personal income scale as they are in the percentage of their population living in urban areas. A similar pattern exists in terms of percentage of personal incomes derived from the several industries.

These relatively backward economic areas in the United States on a map take the shape of a crescent encompassing the South, the Southwest, and the mountain regions of the country. The country's more advanced areas are located in the vast manufacturing belt stretching from the East to the Mid-West and the far West. These areas constitute the most industrialized-urbanized regions of the country.

V. CONCLUSIONS

It would seem that the various regions of the United States tend to be more similar than different. Thus the evidence, such as it is, does not strongly support Professor Nicholls' hypothesis. Relative economic backwardness is shared by regions other than the South. In fairness to Nicholls' hypothesis, however, it should be noted that the South, defined as the 5th and 6th District, is in fact at the bottom of the economic heap. Moreover, if the "South" is defined more broadly so as to include the 8th, 10th and 11th Districts his hypothesis, obviously, gains additional support. On the other hand such a definition is really stretching the point since it would indeed be difficult to label all of these regions as carriers of a "Southern tradition." Could we seriously consider, for example, the 10th District as a part of the "South?"

The evidence is consistent with the hypothesis that the locational matrices of development are primarily industrial-urban rather than rural in composition. So also is the evidence consistent with the hypothesis that relatively under-developed regions of the economy tend to fare better in boom years such as characterized most of those of the decade of the 1950's. It is also true that in this decade the monetary straight-jacket was loosened. Monetary ease in effect contributed to these boom years.

CHAPTER 4

CONTEMPORARY COMMERCIAL BANKING

I. BUSINESS OF BANKING

Contemporary commercial banks may be described as financial department stores. Although banks provide many services to the community, their principal business is the lending and investing of money and handling deposits. This is their "stock and trade." In peddling their wares commercial banks attempt to maximize their returns in a manner similar to all other profit making concerns in the private sector of the economy.

There are two types of returns that a businessman will consider in running his or another's business concern and indeed that an individual will take into account in choosing an occupation. They are pecuniary returns and non-pecuniary returns.

Pecuniary returns are the most easily understood in that they are quantifiable. The information is provided by wage rates, incomes, or from the financial statements of business concerns. The latter for the most part indicate clearly the size of the monetary return that the business organization has managed to obtain from the sale of its products. Non-pecuniary returns, however, are more illusive because they are not readily quantifiable.

In the case of an individual confronted with an occupational choice, for example, non-pecuniary returns depend on his tastes and preferences in evaluating the non-monetary advantages or disadvantages of an occupation. A steady but modest monetary income with congenial co-workers is preferred by some people to the preferences of others for large pecuniary incomes obtainable in more disagreeable surroundings. Similarly, a businessman may prefer a "take things easy" attitude and so a modest monetary return for his organization to the greater exertion that a larger pecuniary return would require. A banker may prefer the "easy life" that safety of greater liquidity offers to the pecuniary income that he will lose through this attitude. And, in fact, moderate but consistent monetary returns is a characteristic of the banking business.

In their attempts to allocate available bank funds so as to maximize monetary and non-monetary returns bankers as businessmen must solve the double problems of liquidity and solvency. At the same time, these problems must be solved within limitations imposed by legal considerations. The amount of liquidity actually needed by an individual bank is of fundamental importance. Too much liquidity means that the bank is foregoing pecuniary returns and thus may not earn what is considered a "normal" return so that stockholders will permanently withdraw their funds from the bank and employ them elsewhere where such a return, or a better one, is obtainable. Too little liquidity, on the other hand, may be fatal to the life of a bank and perhaps disturbing to the banker's peace of mind.

Important that liquidity is to a bank as a going concern it alone cannot guarantee solvency. In this matter banks are not different from other businesses. Thus a business may be liquid enough to meet all its liabilities currently due and for which payment is demanded and still be insolvent. A business concern to be solvent must, at a minimum, possess assets whose total value is as great as the sum of its liabilities to outsiders. And finally, legal considerations impose restrictions on the monetary returns that a bank may earn by limiting its holdings of certain categories of earning assets and excluding others.

II. INPUT "MIX"[1]

As distinct from other businesses, commercial banks take pride in their debt obligations to the public. This is simply from the fact that if bankers had to depend upon their own capital there would indeed be very few banks on the contemporary scene. Deposits (demand and time) are the chief

---

[1] In this chapter I shall adopt David Alhadeff's terminology and refer to deposits as the input of banks and loans and investments as their principal outputs. Such terminology is more accurately descriptive of the similarities among banks and other business enterprises in the private sector of the economy. See David A. Alhadeff, *Monopoly and Competition in Banking* (Berkeley: University of California Press, 1954).

ingredients in the input "mix" of banks. They are used to manufacture the industry's principal product, which is bank credit.

One source of these deposits is the public's surrender of cash to the bank. The second source is the granting of loans and making investments. The first are known as primary deposits and the second as derived deposits. Individual bankers view derived deposits as tending to reduce their cash reserves and so they encourage an increase in primary deposits as a means of enabling them to increase their loan created (or investment created) derived deposits. Thus they attempt to increase confidence in their institution by advertising their debt obligations to present depositors thereby hoping to encourage others to make deposits with them.

The type and nature of the deposit liabilities to the public are important determinants of a bank's input "mix." Commercial bank deposits in the United States may be classified broadly into demand, time, and savings deposits and sub-classified according to the nature of the depositor: (1) private individuals, partnerships, and corporations; (2) states and political subdivisions; (3) United States government; and (4) foreign.

It is generally agreed that classification of deposits according to the functions that they perform does not yield clear lines of demarcation. Demand deposits are typically held for purposes of making payments. Time and savings deposits are an investment outlet for individual savers. There is, however, considerable interchange in the uses to which the various types of accounts are put thereby blurring the lines drawn between their functions. In addition, banks in practice seldom exercise their right to require advance notice of withdrawals from time and savings deposits by their customers.

As in many other industries, commercial banking is not assured of a steady source of supply for its principal inputs. Private individuals who own and use demand deposits for personal convenience are the most numerous class of demand depositors. A banker can depend on regular withdrawals by this class of depositor. This source of supply, normally, will not cause a banker much concern. Far more important to banks in terms of dollar volume are the deposits of business. Since many businesses have special seasonal and cyclical characteristics, a banker must anticipate and prepare for these deposits withdrawals by adjusting his investment portfolios so as to provide the required amount of liquidity. This may reduce the output of his principal product, namely, loans.

Local, state and national government deposits are another source of particular concern to bankers because receipts and expenditures by various levels of government are not synchronized. For instance, at certain times of the year when taxes are collected deposits in public accounts increase substantially and decline in other times when expenditures are heavy. Since coincidence between the deposits of taxpayers and recipients of government checks cannot be counted upon by an individual bank, bankers attempt to offset the public accounts they hold by a high degree of liquidity in their assets and so reduce loan output.

The behavior of foreign deposits is perhaps the least predictable. Their behavior is influenced by a wide range of foreign and domestic factors. Bankers are not readily disposed to use these funds in other than highly liquid activities. Most of these accounts are carried by commercial banks in New York City.

Other major sources of bank funds and so ingredients in a bank's input mix are its own capital, including surplus, individual profits and reserves for losses, and funds borrowed from other banks and the Federal Reserve System.

III. OUTPUT "MIX"

A. Loans

Although investments and loans are both important "products" of commercial banks, loans are their primary form of output. A banker with a decided preference for pecuniary returns, will *ceteris paribus,* also prefer this type of output because of its higher pecuniary return. Loan output "mix" consists of short-term commercial loans, term loans, real estate loans, consumer loans, and security loans.

Business firms are the major customers for short-run commercial loans. Demand for this type of loan is very sensitive to economic fluctuations rising during the upswing of economic activity when business is prosperous and declining in the downswing. Coupled with its cyclical sensitivity is its seasonal variation. There is a tendency for business to increase its bank borrowing to finance the processing of the year's crop and to prepare for holiday shopping. There is also a tendency for business borrowing from banks to be directly related to inventory fluctuations. Inventory build-up or depletion will tend to be reflected in business borrowing.

Term loans are usually sought by businesses that are too small to use capital markets, or by larger firms that prefer to seek term credit from banks rather than to sell their securities. And, indeed, some loans that are classified as "short term" because they are renewed periodically are in fact used by borrowers to finance permanent working capital requirements so that they are in effect term loans.

Real estate loans in the form of farm and non-farm mortgages tend to be the province of small banks. Such loans are a minor "output" of large commercial banks. Demand for this type of loan appears to be independent of moderate movements in general economic activity. Residential construction tends to depend mainly upon family formation, population growth and population shifts. Commercial construction on the other hand is more closely related to movements in general economic activity. Farm mortgages tend to be closely associated with the purchase of land which is influenced by the movement of agricultural prices.

Consumer loans are another important element in the output mix of commercial banks. Moreover, banks meet consumer demands for loans also in an indirect manner. They finance consumers indirectly through loans to dealers in durable goods, sales finance companies, as well as other lending agencies. These loans tend to conform closely to movements in general economic activity. In addition, they appear to be affected by the willingness of consumers to increase their debt which in turn appears to be influenced by evaluation of their past and future incomes.

Security loans are another element in a bank's loan output mix. These loans fall into broad categories: (1) "Street loans," e.g., brokers and dealers in securities; (2) loans made to others for the purpose of carrying securities. This type of lending constitutes an important element in the output mix of banks located in the country's principal financial centers. For most other banks in the country, however, this type of loan is a minor element in their loan output. Demand for security loans is affected primary by changes in stock prices, current margin requirements in stocks and general new security offerings, prevailing rates on security loans, and on speculative activity in the securities markets.

B.   Investment Output

Investments are the other major element in a bank's output mix. In terms of banking history in the United States investment output, as represented by substantial security holdings is a relatively recent development. During World War I security holdings by banks increased and continued to expand into the 1920's. A brief interruption occurred in this development during 1930-33 but thereafter the increase proceeded at an accelerated pace. Commercial bank investments increased and reached a peak of almost 100 billion dollars during World War II.

The investment output mix of commercial banks consists of various types of security holdings by banks. Corporate bonds, municipal securities, and Government securities represent the principal holdings. Relatively unimportant to banks are corporate bonds. Increased construction of various public projects by municipalities and states following World War II has resulted in a market rise in their borrowing. The satisfactory condition of local and state finances coupled with the increased vulnerability of commercial banks to Federal income taxes and the tax exempt features of local securities has resulted in a substantial holding of such securities by a commercial bank.

Holdings of U. S. Government securities are by far the most important item in commercial banking's investment output. During World War II the amount of these securities outstanding exceeded the amount that apparently could be readily absorbed by the non-bank public. Commercial banks with the aid of the Federal Reserve System, which provided them with sufficient reserves, absorbed the balance. Although banks continue to hold government securities, their importance in bank portfolios has tended to decline since 1951 following the "accord" between the Federal Reserve System and the Treasury.

IV.   PRICING OF INPUTS AND OUTPUTS

A.   Pricing Inputs

Deposits are the most important raw material in the production of bank loans and investments. Commercial banks pay for these raw materials either through interest on time deposits or implicitly through remission of service charges on demand or checking deposits. Bankers have attempted to attract primary deposits in still other ways that do not involve direct payment for these raw materials. Architectual design of their banking establishments in the past has attempted to convey the solidity and solemnity of a Greek temple. In the postwar period, however, such design has given way to a more "up to date" approach giving banking establishments a modernistic flair. There is also a tendency to replace or move out of public view the more "priestly" members of the banking fraternity and substitute in their place a "folksy" banker.

Banks have engaged in savings promotion campaigns such as the presentation of miniature vaults to the family offspring.   Added services to the public such as "drive-in banking" and extension of services to the suburbs are additional cases in point. And recently, in some areas, banks have started to serve coffee to their morning customers.   Additional examples of non-price competition in banking are readily available.

To what do we owe these "forward" strides in banking? Perhaps the most important sponsor of non-price competition for the raw materials of banking has been the Banking Act of 1933. Although this Act in many respects is an advancement in American monetary and banking thought, its sponsorship of non-price competition in banking leaves much to be desired. While ostensibly protecting the public against bank failures, the Act has almost frozen commercial banking into the mold of the 1930's. Under its sponsorship banks are prohibited from paying interest on demand deposits. Furthermore, limits on interest rate payments set by the Board of Governors on time deposits closed the route of escape for the banker whose preference may have been for price competition. Government intervention and enforcement was the logical outcome of earlier attempts by local clearing houses to set "standards" that flavored of monopoly. It is usually agreed that a monopoly worthy of the name cannot exist for very long unless the government's police powers are marshalled for its preservation. Attempts by clearing houses to impose on local bankers such "standards" as: (1) maximum rates of interest to be paid in deposits; (2) banking hours and banking holidays; (3) prevention of multiple loans to costomers; (4) uniform charges on services, were doomed to failure unless backed up with something more than threats.

In their attempts to set "standards" by reducing competition among its members, clearing houses are similar to trade associations. A ready example is provided by the American Medical Association that has had a long and apparently unsuccessful battle with "witch doctors," "quacks," and "do it yourself remedies."[2] The Association achieved a measure of success when it obtained government support for its requirement that medical doctors be certified by members of its own fraternity — similar in effect to that required of plumbers by the local plumbers' union. That Scot surgeon and economist Adam Smith may not have been far off target when he warned almost two hundred years ago:

> People of the same trade seldom meet together, even for merriment and diversion but the conversation ends in a conspiracy against the public, or in some contrivance to raise prices.[3]

B. Pricing Output

Loans and investments are major elements in a bank's output mix and also its principal sources of revenue. Service charges on checking accounts and fees and commissions earn-

---

[2] See the study by Milton Friedman and Simon Kuznets, *Income From Independent Practice* (New York: National Bureau of Economic Research, 1954).

[3] Adam Smith, *Wealth of Nations* (New York: Modern Library, Inc., 1937) p. 128.

ed for services rendered customers are minor revenue sources. The bulk of a bank's revenues are, in effect, the product of the interest rate paid by its customers and the total volume of credit that a bank makes available.

Pricing of bank output by the banking industry differs in one important respect from practices usually followed by other industries in selling their products. The latter tend to confront their customers with established prices and terms of sales thereby-permitting the exercise of consumer's choice. Banking industry, however, does not present its customers with established prices and other terms of sale. Each loan is individually negotiated between borrower and banker. Since each loan is likely to differ in its various details the banker is apparently presented with a greater opportunity to exercise price discrimination than producers of other products.

A banker will take into consideration a number of factors in quoting a loan rate to a borrower.[4] For example, he will consider the financial size of the borrower or loan, the quality and type of credit, duration of loan, the nature and degree of risk, cost of administering the loan, competition among banks, the type of collateral, the borrower's average balances maintained at the bank, the importance of the account to the bank and the character of the banker-customer relation. Perhaps the most important determinant of loan rates, however, is the availability of alternative sources of supply to the borrower. Borrowers with no alternative sources of supply for their credit needs are often at the mercy of the local bankers.

Scattered evidence seems to suggest that it is the relatively small or medium size business that tends to pay a higher price for the banking industry's product. This may be attributed to the fact that a given size loan usually implies given conditions of risk, costs of administration of the loan, size of balances, and general worth to the bank. The net effect of these factors is that rates charged by banks tend to vary inversely with the size of loan. Since the loan requirements of small and medium size businesses are relatively modest,

[4] David A. Alhadeff, *Monopoly and Competition in Banking* (Berkeley: University of California Press, 1954) p. 112.

their rates would be expected to be higher than those paid
by large business enterprises. At the same time, a large business enterprise has many alternate sources of supply at its
disposal. Such an opportunity is seldom available to a modest
business concern. Governor Young summarized the extent of
these opportunities in the 1930's in testimony before a Congressional Committee.

> For instance, let us take a small community in South
> Dakota: A farmer who has to borrow $1,000 or
> $2,000 is known to the local banker and not known
> to anyone else. He cannot go to New York, Vermont
> or Maine and present his vote. No one knows him.
> Therefore, he has to pay the legal rate or contract
> rate . . . [of, say] 10 per cent. That is the rate he
> would probably have to pay to the local bank unless
> he was well enough known so he could go to a nearby
> town with a very desirable piece of paper and drive
> a bargain, say, for 8 per cent.[5]

If we take the statements of official banking spokesmen
seriously, they indicate that the banking mentality is dominated by the spirit of no price competition.   Thus, one
spokesman declared before a Congressional Committee:

> This competition between banks is in quality of ser-
> vice; . . . there is seldom a question of price; . . .
> there is no real problem of cheaper banking for us
> to solve.[6]

And another spokesman stated: "Banks have no bargains
to offer, no cut rates."[7]
Interesting though such statements may be, they should
not be taken literally. In analysis it is more important to
determine what people, including bankers, actually do than
what they say they do. Silly questions deserve silly answers.
The argument is similar to the view that oligopolies and monopolies cause inflation by "administering prices." It is assert-

---

[5] Hearings before the Committee on Banking and Currency, H.R., 71st
Cong., 2nd Sess., *Branch, Chain and Group Banking*, Vol. I, p. 709. Also cited
by Alhadeff, *op. cit.*, p. 23.
[6] Alhadeff, *op. cit.*, p. 22.
[7] *Ibid.*, p. 22.

ed that "administered prices" are more authoritatively determined than competitive prices, and hence are excellent conductors of inflationary pressure. Many economists, on the other hand, argue that administered prices are not so rigid as they seem.[8] It is held that during periods when the state of demand is favorable they do not rise so rapidly as competitive prices, and thus, in effect, they may well be below levels that would clear the market, thereby creating lists and gray markets. When administered prices do rise, however, they are likely to do so in large jumps, thus attracting charges that they are "responsible" for inflation.

A number of other factors appear to be more important than alleged customer discrimination and non-price competition in limiting the ability of commercial banks to service the needs of their principal customers — the small and medium size business. Some of these factors are related to the nature of commercial banking and others to the pattern of public regulation that has restricted its operations.[9]

In the past bank lending has been conducted on the assumption that instability will tend to characterize the American economy. Accordingly, individual bankers will not assume ordinary risks if there is danger that the economy will be subject to sharp economic fluctuations. Moreover, selectivity of risks by banks is attributable to the fact that banks have a relatively small cushion of equity.

The short term and unstable character of deposit liabilities force bankers to seek assets that will enable them to meet their liabilities under all foreseeable conditions. Even though bankers have an opportunity to borrow from the Federal Reserve System in the event of deposit withdrawal, they have concerned themselves, and according to some, excessively, about the composition and stability of their deposit liabilities. Tradition and concern lest such borrowing cast doubt on their credit position has made commercial banks averse to borrowing at the Federal Reserve System.

---

[8] See George Macesich, "The Joint Economic Committee's Study of Inflation," *Social Research*, Autumn 1962, pp. 357-379.
[9] Neil H. Jacoby and Raymond J. Saulnier, *Business Finance and Banking* (New York: National Bureau of Research, 1948) pp. 209ff.

And on this score the Federal Reserve System has done little to allay their fears.

Laws and administrative regulation are also factors limiting risk taking on the part of banks. Banks are not permitted to underwrite security issues either directly or indirectly. They may not hold obligations of any one obligor in amounts exceeding 10 per cent of a bank's capital and surplus account. Moreover, examination of bank loan portfolios by government examiners has affected the readiness of commercial banks to make innovations in their business lending policies. And finally, usury laws have resulted in reluctance on the part of bankers to lend money at rates in excess of "standard" or "conventional" bank rates. One consequence is that some banks turn customers away rather than charge "excessive" rates while others evade the law by employing service charges and other means to raise the gross interest rate.

V. ECONOMIC ENVIRONMENT

To judge from the hypotheses discussed in Chapters 1 and 2 and the above discussion, we should expect to observe that commercial banks not only influence but are themselves in turn influenced by the economic environment in which they operate. Thus, one implication of Professor Nicholls' hypothesis is that the acceptance of all fine elements of his "Southern tradition" by Southern bankers would have the effect, among other things, of generating a higher liquidity preference among them than bankers elsewhere in the country. The Southern banker would prefer the safety and convenience of greater liquidity to the income he will lose through this attitude. Moreover, such an attitude may be reinforced by a desire to preserve other elements of the Southern tradition. The new "industrial upstarts" would be prevented from upsetting the existing *status quo* if only because Southern bankers allocate and hold a smaller proportion of their assets in the form of loans. These bankers, however, would be derelict in carrying out the principal function of commercial banking which is the production of loans. If this hypothesis is correct, then, all other things equal, Southern bankers share much of the responsibility for impeding the South's economic development and preserving its "tradition."

The hypotheses advanced by Schultz, Clark, Ratchford and MacDonald all have similar implications for banking. We should expect to observe that returns to commercial banking are in fact inversely associated with the degree of economic development in the region.

The implications of Dunn's hypothesis for banking appear to be straightforward. Southern banking, all other things equal, should also be slow growth since by and large it is servicing a region dominated by slow growth industries. Accordingly, we should expect to observe that all other things equal, returns to Southern banking are lower relative to other more developed regions.

Subsequent chapters will test the empirical consistency of these hypotheses against commercial banking data in the several Federal Reserve Districts.

CHAPTER 5

A SURVEY OF CHANGES IN THE STRUCTURE
OF COMMERCIAL BANKING IN SOUTHERN STATES
1950-60

I. INSTITUTIONAL FRAMEWORK: STATE BANKING LAWS

A.   Deposit Insurance

Banking laws are important determinants of the structure of banking in the South as they are elsewhere.[1] As we
would expect these laws in the South have many characteristics common to the rest of the country. One common characteristic is that states chartering banks in their territories
require banks to insure the funds of depositors. And indeed
banking laws in the South are so framed that a prospective
bank usually must meet the requirements of the Federal Deposit Insurance Corporation (FDIC), which, as elsewhere,
is the region's primary insuring agency, before a charter is
considered.

Evidence summarized in Table 5.1 suggests the extent to
which Southern banks are insured. Excluding Georgia, the
region's record for the percentage of banks insured is slightly
better than for the United States as a whole. Georgia is the
only state which has a sizeable proportion of its banks not
insured by the FDIC. In fact, the state's banks constitute
70.7 per cent of all noninsured banks in the South. Many
of these banks not insured by the FDIC are insured by
other agencies and when acccount is taken of this fact, only
13.8 per cent of Georgia's banks are not insured. Such banks,
however, are primarily unincorporated banks operating outside the definition of state banks found in the FDIC Act.[2]

---

* I am indebted to Mr. Jan Duggar for many of the compilations and sum-
maries presented in this chapter and its appendix.
[1] The Southern states reviewed in this chapter are Alabama, Florida, Georgia, Louisiana, Maryland, Mississippi, North Carolina, South Carolina, Tennessee, Virginia and West Virginia. This is a broader definition of the "South"
than the 5th and 6th Federal Reserve Districts which is used throughout this
study.
[2] Annual Report 1960, F.D.I.C. (Washington: Government Printing Office,
1961) p. 92.

Table 5.1

Number of Banks by State and Insurance Category

State	Total Banks	Insured	Non-insured	Percentage Insured
Alabama	238	238	—	100.0
Florida	309	304	5	99.3
Georgia	421	363	58	86.2
Louisiana	190	189	1	99.5
Maryland	139	137	2	98.6
Mississippi	193	191	2	99.0
North Carolina	183	181	1	99.5
South Carolina	145	139	6	95.9
Tennessee	297	291	6	99.0
Virginia	305	305	—	100.0
West Virginia	182	181	1	99.5
South	2,602	2,520	82	97.8
United States	13,999	13,451	548	96.5

Source: Annual report of the Federal Deposit Insurance Corporation for the
year ended December 31, 1960 (Washington, D.C.: Government
Printing Office, 1961) Table 103, pp. 128-135.

Another common characteristic of state laws is that
banks are, for example, permitted to issue stock, receive
deposits and make loans. In short, state banking laws tend
not to differ in according banks rights to engage in various
activities normally associated with the industry.

Organization of authority governing banking in the
several states, however differs. Although in many of the
Southern states a commissioner of banking is appointed by the governor of the state with Senate approval,
in Florida, Mississippi, South Carolina, and in Virginia a different procedure exists. Thus in Florida and in
Mississippi the State Comptroller has power over state chartered banks; in South Carolina such power rests with the
State Board of Control headed by the State Treasurer; and

in Virginia the State Corporate Commission supervises the state chartered banks. An appendix to this chapter surveys the banking laws of the several Southern states.

B. Branch Banking

The principal banking differences amongst the several states arise from the treatment accorded branch banking. Information summarized in Table 5.2 indicates that only three Southern states permit state-wide branch banking while six permit limited area branch banking and two permit only unit banking.

It is interesting to compare percentagewise the status of branch banking in the Southern states and in the country as a whole. Such a comparison yields results which suggest that there is a higher concentration of branch banking systems in the South than in the rest of the country. Thus the eleven Southern states account for 21.4 per cent of the total continental states with a statewide branch system; they account for 37.5 of the states with limited-area branch banking; and Southern states with unit bank systems account for only 11.1 per cent of the total states with such a banking system.

Table 5.2

Classification of Southern States According to Branch and Unit Banking

State-Wide Branch Banking	Limited Area Branch Banking[1]		Unit Banking
Maryland	Louisiana	Tennessee	Florida[2]
North Carolina	Oklahoma	Georgia	West Virginia
South Carolina	Mississippi	Virginia	

Source: Appendix to Chapter 5.

[1] Branch banking is limited by parish in Louisiana, by county in Tennessee, Alabama, Mississippi, and Virginia, and by city and area populaton in Georgia.

[2] Although Florida was restricted to unit banking in 1960, for example, 14 branch banks operated on military bases in the State.

Even in those Southern states where limited branch banking only is permitted, bankers have found ways to circumvent such restrictions. Virginia is a good case in point. Branch banking in the state is restricted to the city or county in which the parent bank is located. The law, however, permits a bank to merge with any bank in an adjoining county or within twenty-five miles of the head office, provided both banks have existed for five years. A way is thus provided for a parent bank to sponsor or indeed "plant" a unit bank for a five year period, after which a merger can occur and the parent bank can operate its "plant" as a branch. Still other ways are available. Thus in unit bank states, for example, banks may petition the state supervisory authorities for permission to open a limited branch bank or military or other government installations. This has been the case in Florida which is a unit bank state.

Some idea of the significance that banking laws have in shaping the structure of banking is indicated by the fact that in the South about 80 per cent of all branch banks are new offices constructed for area banking. The remaining 20 per cent are created by bank mergers. This latter method is more desirable from the standpoint of a bank desiring branches since it is quick and relatively inexpensive. As the evidence in Table 5.3 suggests in those states permitting statewide branch banking between 50 and 73 per cent of all bank offices are branch banks. In states permitting limited area branch banking, between 20 and 48 per cent of all banking offices are branch banks. If the South is defined as the Fifth and Sixth Federal Reserve Districts, statewide branch banking systems are concentrated in the Fifth District.

The increase in the face of urbanization and concomitant growth of suburbs occuring in the South (Fifth and Sixth Federal Reserve Districts) in the decade 1950-60 has in fact been responsible for the rapid rise in branch offices. This is especially true for the period since 1955 according to the evidence summarized in Table 5.3. Thus, for the period 1950-55 a 4 per cent increase in branch banks occurred while for the period 1955-60 a 13 per cent increase in registered States permitting some form of branch banking have enabled Southern bankers to extend their operations into suburban

Table 5.3

Percentage of Banks and Branch Offices by States, Selected Years 1950-1960

State	Branches as Percent of Bank Offices			Percent Increase in Bank Offices	Percent Increase in Banks
	1950	1955	1960	1950-60	1950-60
Alabama	10.35	16.54	27.43	30.67	5.77
Florida	2.92	4.80	4.33	57.56	55.27
Georgia	9.56	13.03	20.11	20.04	6.04
Louisiana	31.81	40.06	48.08	51.23	15.15
Maryland	43.83	54.80	67.06	37.01	-19.65
Mississippi	25.27	33.22	41.33	22.30	- 3.98
North Carolina	49.20	54.69	73.51	55.98	-18.66
South Carolina	24.87	36.59	50.34	48.22	- 2.02
Tennessee	24.81	31.57	42.10	29.87	0.00
Virginia	26.69	35.97	48.21	37.93	- 2.55
West Virginia	0.00	0.00	0.00	1.11	1.11
Fifth Federal Reserve District	33.18	42.08	56.15	39.93	- 8.18
Sixth Federal Reserve District	17.60	23.34	30.95	32.37	11.05
South	25.71	29.73	42.96	35.93	3.13
United States	25.98	34.09	43.57	26.46	- 8.45

Source: Computed from *Annual Reports* of the Federal Deposit Insurance Corporation for years ending December 31, 1950, 1955, and 1960.

business centers. At the same time they have made it more difficult for units banks to locate in such centers. Insofar as the customer is concerned, however, branch banks appear to have a slight edge over unit banks in that a parent bank can more easily open a branch in a suburban area prior to that time when a unit bank would find it profitable to enter the area.

This would suggest that branch banking tends to restrict entry into the industry. Thus the evidence presented in Table 5.4 indicates that although in the South as a whole there has been an increase in the number of national and non-member banks the increase can be accounted for largely by Sixth Federal Reserve District. And in this District the unit bank state of Florida accounts for most of the increase in the number of banks. In the branch banking state of North Carolina, on the other hand, the number of banks decreased by forty-two in the period 1951-60 even though not a single bank failure occurred in this period. What happened, of course, is that these forty-two banks were absorbed by other

Table 5.4

Net change in the number of National Banks, State Member Banks, and State Non-member Banks, 1951-1960

	National Banks	State Member Banks	State Non-member Banks
Alabama	- 1	1	12
Florida	56	- 1	45
Georgia	2	- 4	25
Louisiana	8	0	18
Maryland	- 9	- 8	15
Mississippi	3	1	-11
North Carolina	- 10	- 5	-27
South Carolina	0	- 1	6
Tennessee	1	- 2	1
Virginia	- 4	- 2	- 4
West Virginia	3	- 1	2
Fifth Federal Reserve District	- 20	- 17	- 8
Sixth Federal Reserve District	69	- 5	90
South	49	- 22	82
United States	-409	-257	337

Source: Computed from *Annual Reports* of the Federal Deposit Insurance Corporation for years ending December 31, 1951-1960.

banks and for the most part became branches. The story is much the same in Virginia and Maryland.

Such restrictions on entry are facilitated by the apparent cost advantages of branch banks over unit banks. To judge from available studies operating costs in branch banking systems are significantly lower than those in unit banking systems.[3] Such savings as are derived, for example, from a centralized research department, a staff of specialists, and relatively expensive machinery are not as readily available to small unit banks. But whether or not these cost reductions are transferred to bank customers is another matter.

A branch banking system, however, may have advantages to the region in which it is located. According to its supporters such a system facilitates the movement of funds into, and for that matter out of, various economic or geographic areas. Moreover, the exchange of investments amongst the various banks in a branch enables them to diversify their portfolios sufficiently without the necessity of going into the open market to secure diversification.[4] The net effect is that a branch banking system serves as a method for mobilizing liquidity. A branch bank, for example, may safely leave provisions for liquidity in charge of its parent bank. A unit bank, however, is not so fortunate. This is a problem it must solve for itself and in search of a solution a unit bank may not be able to "see the forest for the trees." As a result a unit bank may maintain a liquidity position equal to that of a parent bank in a branch system. If so, a considerable amount of a community's resources would be immobilized by a unit banking system than would tend to be the case with a branch banking system. Some relief from such a possibility is available through membership in the Federal Reserve System. But then this is possible for a branch banking system as well. More will be said later regarding member banks of the Federal Reserve System.

C. Capital Requirements

Legally specified capital requirements based on city population are another important difference amongst the several

---

[3] See for example, David A. Alhadeff, *Monopoly and Competition in Banking* (Berkeley: University of California Press, 1954).

[4] *Ibid.*, pp. 65-66.

Southern states. Data in Table 5.5 summarize by state and city population capital requirements. The net effect of capital requirements in the various states is not clear cut owing to the influence of many other factors.

Consider, for example, the effect of state capital requirements on the number of banks. All other things equal, we should expect to observe that capital requirements and the number of banks will vary inversely. It is obvious, however, that "all other things" are seldom equal. Thus, for example, Georgia and Mississippi have the lowest capital requirements of any of the Southern states. Georgia also has the largest number of banks of any state in the South. Mississippi, on the other hand, with the same capital requirements has experienced a decline in the number of banks but a sharp increase in the number of branch bank offices. In both states

Table 5.5

Capital Requirements by State
(In Thousands)

State	Population of City (in 000)							
	3	5	10	25	50	100	150	200
Alabama	$25	$50	$100	$100	$200	$200	$200	$200
Florida	25	25	50	100	200	200	200	200
Georgia	25	25	50	50	50	50	50	50
Louisiana	25	50	50	50	100	100	100	100
Maryland	25	25	25	75	100	100	500	500
Mississippi	25	25	50	50	50	50	50	50
North Carolina	50	75	100	125	150	150	150	150
South Carolina	25	50	100	100	100	100	100	100
Tennessee	50	75	75	100	200	200	200	200
Virginia	50	50	50	50	62.5	87.5	112.5	137.5
West Virginia	25	50	100	100	150	150	150	150
National Banks	50	50	100	100	200	200	200	200

Source: Appendix to this Chapter.

limited branch banking is permitted. The unit bank state of Florida has experienced a rapid increase in the number of banks even though stiff capital requirements are in force in the state. Florida also has the highest population per bank in the country.

D.   Other Requirements and Restrictions

Various other requirements and restrictions are imposed on banks by the states. For example, the amount that can be loaned to any one borrower is based on a bank's aggregate capital and ranges from 10 to 20 per cent of such capital. Restrictions on maximum rates of interest that banks may charge are another factor restricting a bank's operations. In all Southern states the maximum rate is 6 per cent in Georgia and Louisiana where 8 per cent is permissable. Reserve requirements are another restriction imposed by states and range from 25 per cent of demand deposits and 10 per cent of time deposits in Mississippi to a low of 7 per cent of demand dposits and 3 per cent of time deposits in South Carolina.

Many Southern states also require their chartered banks to set aside a surplus fund from yearly profits ranging from 20 per cent of capital in most states to 100 per cent of capital in Mississippi. Still another type of restriction is that imposed by North Carolina which requires a surplus fund equal to 50 per cent of authorized capital to be paid prior to the opening of the bank. On the other hand, two other states, West Virginia and Tennessee, have no state surplus fund requirements. Other laws in the several states restrict the maximum rate of exchange and the minimum rate per check a bank may charge.

But of all the various state banking laws, the requirements on branch banking appear to be the most important in determining the structure of a state's banking system. There are other factors that may be as important but their influences are not as clear cut. Amongst these, considerations should be given to the policies of the State Banking Commission and the human and natural resources of the state. The comparatively heavy concentration of branch banking systems in the South is mute testimony to the willingness of many people, especially bankers to "experiment" with arrangements considered by some to smack of monopoly.

II. CONCENTRATION

The high mortality of banks during the 1920's and early 1930's stimulated bank mergers as a defensive measure. A steady decline in the number of commercial banks in the United States is indicated in the period 1934-61. In fact, the decline in the number of banks for the country as a whole averages about ½ per cent per year. On the other hand, the South has gained in the number of banks at an average rate of about 3 per cent per year.

If the South is divided into the Fifth and Sixth Federal Reserve Districts the source of this increase is clearly indicated. Thus conditions in the Fifth District are about on par with those in other parts of the country favoring branch banking. The Sixth District, on the other hand, accounts for most of the South's increase in the number of banks. And within the District the unit bank state of Florida with an average annual increase of 5 per cent in the number of banks is primarily responsible for the increased number of banks.

The evidence summarized in Table 5.6 suggests that the decline in the number of banks is accompanied by an increase in the population per bank. Population per bank office for the year 1934 and 1958 indicate the extent to which mergers have occurred. According to recent reports in 85 per cent of all mergers the acquired banks were converted into branches.[5] For the most part the absorbed banks were small size organizations with deposits of 5 million dollars or less. The acquiring banks, on the other hand, tended to be large size organizations with deposits over 50 million dollars.

It is also of interest to note that in the states permitting branch banking there has been a decrease in population per *bank office* and an increase in population per *bank*. In Florida, on the other hand, there has been an increase in population per bank office and bank during the period of study (1950-60) owing, as already noted, to the unit bank requirements of the state's banking laws.

---

[5] Charlotte P. Alhadeff and David A. Alhadeff, "Recent Bank Mergers," *The Quarterly Journal of Economics*, November 1955, p. 511.

Table 5.6

Population Per Bank and Per Bank Office by State 1934 and 1958

State	Population Per Bank		Population Per Bank Office	
	1934	1958	1934	1958
Alabama	12,353	13,435	11,529	10,668
Florida	10,573	15,864	10,434	15,160
Georgia	8,787	9,312	8,144	7,856
Louisiana	14,872	16,720	10,916	9,094
Maryland	8,532	19,839	5,755	7,579
Mississippi	9,798	11,268	8,415	6,874
North Carolina	13,602	22,409	10,555	7,397
South Carolina	13,609	16,694	11,384	8,839
Tennessee	8,228	11,641	7,175	7,212
Virginia	7,729	12,612	6,396	7,207
West Virginia	10,028	10,760	9,972	10,760
United States	7,974	12,561	6,643	7,498

Source: *Annual Report* of the F.D.I.C. for year ending December 31, 1960, p. 42.

If the concentration of deposits is considered, available evidence presented in Table 5.7 suggests that there is a heavy concentration of the region's deposits in the hands of one to five large banks located in metropolitan areas. Within thirteen principal metropolitan areas of the South, for example, five local banks hold the bulk of all local deposits. And indeed in eleven of these areas one bank holds between 30 to 60 per cent of all deposits and five of the largest banks account for 88 to 100 per cent of all local deposits.

Table 5.7

Deposits in the Largest Banks in the Principal Counties in
Metropolitan Areas, December 31, 1958

Metropolitan Area	Percent of Deposits Held by the Largest Bank	Percent of Deposits Held by the Five Largest Banks
Birmingham: Jefferson County, Alabama	62.1	98.8
Norfolk-Portsmouth: Norfolk County, Virginia	56.3	97.2
Knoxville: Knox County, Tennessee	50.4	100.0
Memphis: Shelby County, Tennessee	45.5	97.2
Atlanta: DeKalb and Fulton Counties, Georgia	44.5	89.7
New Orleans: Orleans County, Louisiana	41.6	99.7
Nashville: Davidson County, Tennessee	39.8	98.9
Richmond: Henrico County, Virginia	31.3	94.9
Wheeling-Steubenville, Ohio County, West Virginia	41.0	91.0
Charleston: Kanawha County, West Virginia	32.9	88.3
Jacksonville: Duval County, Florida	31.9	89.5
Miami: Dade County, Florida	27.5	53.3
Tampa-St. Petersburg, Pinellas-Hillsborough Counties, Florida	15.6	57.8

Source: *Annual Report* of the F.D.I.C. for year ending December 31, 1960.

As would be expected in states permitting state-wide branch banking there is a high concentration of total deposits in a few banks. To judge from the evidence summarized in Table 5.8 in those states with branch banking one bank controls between 12 and 25 per cent of all deposits within the state and the five largest banks hold between 40 to 50 per cent of the deposits in the state.

Table 5.8

Deposits in the Largest Commercial Bank, and in the Largest Five Commercial Banks in Each State, 1940 and 1958

State	Total Banks	Percent of Deposits in the Largest Bank		Percent of Deposits in the Five Largest Banks	
		1940	1958	1940	1958
Branch Banking					
Maryland	132	29.5	12.7	55.3	48.8
North Carolina	163	20.5	20.6	48.4	47.1
South Carolina	144	25.2	25.3	51.3	51.1
Limited Branch Banking					
Alabama	238	21.4	18.2	54.5	40.8
Georgia	420	24.1	17.3	61.7	48.1
Louisiana	192	26.1	15.2	59.1	39.6
Mississippi	193	6.9	11.8	22.2	28.3
Tennessee	294	13.8	11.2	48.7	40.3
Virginia	302	12.1	7.5	35.2	27.5
Unit Banking					
Florida	315	14.0	6.8	42.6	21.0
West Virginia	181	7.7	6.5	30.0	24.3

Source: *Annual Report* of the F.D.I.C. for year ending December 31, 1960, p. 54.

III. NON-PAR BANKS

So-called non-par banks tend to be smaller than par remitting banks and located in one bank "small-towns." These banks tend to have a lower ratio of earning total assets than

par-remitting banks of the same size. According to some students, non-par banks do not manage their funds as "efficiently" as par remitting banks because they tend to "forego" investment income averaging up to 50 per cent of their exchange
income.[6] Moreover, non-par banks typically do not compete
with other banks. When a par-remitting bank locates in the
same town, however, the situation is different and non-par
banks are forced to also remit at par. Apparently without
such competition non-par banks are content to continue to levy
exchanges charges.[7]

The South has a comparatively large percentage of non-
par banks reflecting, in effect, a large number of one bank
towns. In December 1961 in the Fifth and Sixth Federal Reserve Districts there were respectively 909 and 1,382 banks.
Of these banks, 31 in the Fifth District and 546 in the Sixth
District were non-par remitting banks. Indeed the South
contains only 17.2 per cent of the total banks in the country
but 41.4 per cent of all the country's non-par banks.

The two Carolinas in the Fifth District account for most
of the non-par banks in the District. The situation, however,
is worse in the sixth District where 45 per cent of total banks
are non-par. The evidence presented in Table 5.9 locates
these banks by states. Georgia and Mississippi have the largest concentrations of non-par banks suggesting the rather
limited competition prevailing in the banking industry in
these two states except in metropolitan areas.

Non-par remitting banks tend to be a drag on the economic development of communities in which they are located.
An industry with a large payroll and in need of bank services
will hesitate in locating in a community where it will be
be penalized for making its transactions by check.

IV. SIZE OF BANKS, DISTRIBUTION OF COMMERCIAL BANK
     ASSETS AND LIABILITIES

A. Federal Reserve System and Bank Asset Size

The importance of the Federal Reserve System to Southern banking and thus to the region's development is apparent

---

[6] Clifton H. Kreps, Jr., "Characteristics of Nonpar Banking: A Case Study,"
Southern Economic Journal, July 1959, p. 49 .
[7] *Ibid.*, p. 49.

Table 5.9

Number of Nonpar Banks and Percentage of All Banks, 1950 and 1960

State	1950		1960	
	Number of Nonpar	Percent Nonpar	Number of Nonpar	Percent Nonpar
Alabama	96	43	83	35
Florida	61	32	42	14
Georgia	284	72	281	67
Louisiana	104	63	108	57
Maryland	0	0	0	0
Mississippi	161	80	139	72
North Carolina	113	54	75	43
South Carolina	88	58	68	47
Tennessee	91	31	78	26
Virginia	3	2	1	1
West Virginia	1	1	0	0
Fifth Federal Reserve District	307	21	146	17
Sixth Federal Reserve District	796	54	731	45
United States	1,868	13	1,673	13

Source: Research Department, *Statistics on the Structure of Commercial Banking in the Sixth Federal Reserve District: 1950 and 1960* (Atlanta: Federal Reserve Bank of Atlanta, 1962) pp. 1-4; and Research Department, *Fifth District Banking in the Fifties* (Richmond: Federal Reserve Bank of Richmond, 1961) p. 60.

when the distribution of commercial bank assets and liabilities amongst the several classes of banks is considered. Nonmember banks tend to hold a higher proportion of their assets in government securities as a liquidity hedge. Such security holdings in the first instance deprive the area of resources which otherwise could be loaned.

Fortunately for the South, however, members of the Federal Reserve System hold the bulk of commercial bank assets and liabilities. Member banks in the Sixth District, for example, accounted for almost 80 per cent of the District's total commercial bank deposits. One significant feature of member banks is that they may borrow from Federal Reserve Banks and thus may maintain a smaller proportion of their assets in such highly liquid form represented by government securities. Thus availability of Federal Reserve support permits a member bank to hold a greater proportion of its assets in less liquid form such as, for example, in loans than in the case of non-member banks where such support is not readily available. Subsequent chapters will discuss earnings, expenses, capital and the distribution of assets amongst member banks in the several Federal Reserve Districts of the country. It should, of course, be noted that since member banks are required to purchase "stocks" of Federal Reserve Banks their lending capacity will tend to be reduced somewhat.

According to the evidence presented in Table 5.10 Florida, of all the Southern states, has the largest amount of bank assets and South Carolina the smallest. Florida banks, however, have only a slightly larger amount of commercial loans out-

Table 5.10

Assets and Selected Loans by State, December 31, 1960

(In Thousands of Dollars)

State	Total Assets	Commercial Loans	Loans to Individuals
Alabama	2,350,272	348,232	333,587
Florida	5,352,301	690,484	688,961
Georgia	3,280,033	502,171	490,670
Louisiana	3,254,143	500,269	273,083
Maryland	2,583,870	285,899	293,918
Mississippi	1,471,598	208,254	141,337
North Carolina	3,298,746	546,365	447,440
South Carolina	1,147,915	153,666	150,642
Tennessee	3,656,479	634,686	534,998
Virginia	3,642,842	435,252	581,688
West Virginia	1,437,598	103,958	201,898

Source: *Assets, Liabilities, and Capital Accounts of Commercial and Mutual Savings Banks,* December 31, 1960, Report No. 54 (Washington: F.D.I.C., 1961) pp. 16-64.

standing than Tennessee banks even though the state has 64 per cent as many bank assets as Florida.

Useful insights into the nature of the region's banking may be had by considering the average size of bank by assets, class and state. Such a breakdown is summarized in Table 5.11. The evidence indicates that Florida, Louisiana, Maryland, and North Carolina all have comparatively large banks. Moreover, in Louisiana, Tennessee, and Georgia the average size of national bank is larger than in the region's other states. The explanation appears straight-forward. There are a few national banks located in each of these states and the bulk are centered in the region's large metropolitan areas such as New Orleans, Atlanta, Memphis, and Nashville.

A wide range of sizes occurs in state banks which are also members of the Federal Reserve System. Thus, for exam-

Table 5.11

Average Size of Bank by Class and State
(In Thousands of Dollars)

State	Average	National Banks	State Member Banks	State Non-member Banks
Alabama	9,875	24,204	6,762	3,571
Florida	17,606	29,288	32,717	8,798
Georgia	9,036	33,485	34,860	3,436
Louisiana	12,217	49,919	20,635	6,842
Maryland	19,574	25,477	45,105	12,826
Mississippi	7,704	15,567	31,146	5,141
New York	132,668	57,313	336,603	32,224
North Carolina	18,124	30,204	274,458	9,706
Ohio	21,446	29,191	31,324	6,356
South Carolina	8,258	28,485	5,192	3,746
Tennessee	12,565	34,056	24,441	4,359
Virginia	11,943	16,197	12,944	6,170
West Virginia	7,942	9,846	10,048	4,824

Source: *Assets, Liabilities, and Capital Accounts of Commercial and Mutual Savings Banks,* December 31, 1960, Report No. 54 (Washington: F.D.I.C. 1961) pp. 16-64.

ple, in North Carolina there are only four state member banks and all are large state branch banking systems and have on the average assets worth over 274 million dollars. On the other hand, South Carolina also with a state wide branch banking system has 26 state member banks with an average asset size of only 5 million dollars. In the state non-member bank class, Maryland holds the lead where the average size bank is the largest.

B.   ASSET TO CAPITAL RATIO

John McFerrin wrote in 1947 that undercapitalization of banks "is more serious in the South than in the other states and constitutes a problem that must be met before Southern banking can make much additional progress."[8] He goes on to state that the percentage increase in total capital in Southern states was increasing at a rate greater than in other states, but that in 1945 the ratio between assets and capital was 21 to 1 in the South against 17 to 1 in the rest of the country. Undercapitalization of banks, however, is no longer a serious problem. In fact, in 1960 the assets to capital ratio for Southern banks is 12 to 1 which compares favorably to such wealthy states as New York and Ohio.

C.   DISTRIBUTION OF ASSETS

To judge from available evidence, Southern banks in 1960 compared favorably with banks elsewhere in the country in the proportion of total assets held in cash and balances with other banks. This ratio ranged from 18.4 to 24.6 per cent for all Southern banks. Their holding of U. S. government securities, a highly liquid asset, ranged from a low 21.9 per cent for Georgia banks to 34.0 per cent for banks in West Virginia. In fact, only three Southern states — Florida (29.5), Maryland (28.4) and West Virginia (34.0) — exceeded the proportion of U.S. Government held by Ohio whose banks held 27.5 per cent of their total assets in this form.

The distribution of assets amongst banks differs according to the class of banks. As we would expect member banks

---

[8] John B. McFerrin, "Resources for Financing Industry in the South," *The Southern Economic Journal*, July 1947, p. 48.

of the Federal Reserve System tend to hold a smaller proportion of their total assets in U.S. government securities than non-member banks. The evidence summarized in Table 5.12 also suggests that member banks tend to hold a greater proportion of their assets in the form of loans and discounts than non-member banks. This suggests the singular importance of member banks and in effect the Federal Reserve System to the region's economic developmnt.

V. BANK EARNINGS

Evidence on the earnings of Southern banks is summarized in Table 5.13. These data present by state and class of bank income per $100 of U.S. government securities, per $100

Table 5.12

Selected Assets by Class of Bank and by State
December 31, 1960

State	United States Government Obligations			Loans and Discounts		
	National Bank	State Member Bank	State Bank	National Bank	State Member Bank	State Bank
Alabama	23.4	30.5	29.1	43.5	38.8	37.8
Florida	27.5	25.3	35.0	36.6	42.4	38.6
Georgia	17.8	18.0	31.0	48.7	49.0	39.8
Louisiana	25.6	23.4	27.4	40.3	41.9	34.7
Maryland	28.1	25.4	29.9	40.0	45.6	46.6
Mississippi	24.0	17.4	24.2	39.7	43.4	36.1
North Carolina	20.0	14.3	24.8	46.1	45.8	42.0
South Carolina	27.5	24.0	25.4	41.9	30.3	37.5
Tennessee	21.4	25.4	22.3	46.0	46.8	45.9
Virginia	24.1	22.7	29.8	46.9	48.3	44.4
West Virginia	35.1	29.4	36.1	37.2	40.5	39.5

Source: *Assets, Liabilities, and Capital Accounts of Commercial and Mutual Savings Banks,* December 31, 1960, Report No. 54 (Washington: F.D.I.C. 1961) pp. 16-64.

of loans, service charges per $100 of deposits, and interest paid per $100 of time and savings deposits. As we would expect non-member banks received the greatest income from U.S. government securities, loans, and service charges. They also paid the highest interest rates on time and savings accounts. Differences in income received and interest paid among the three classes of banks can in part be accounted for by size of banks, composition of loan structure, legal interest rates, and competitive factors within the area in which the bank is located.

The influence of bank size is readily demonstrated in several of the states. Thus, Maryland has the largest size of banks in the South. It also has the lowest average income on loans. Such states as Alabama, Georgia, South Carolina and West Virginia with relatively small sized banks also earned relatively high returns on loans. Thus their returns per $100 of loans in 1960 are $6.26, $6.61, $6.30 and $6.27 respectively or percentagewise 6.26%, 6.61%, 6.30% and 6.27%; Maryland banks, on the other hand, obtained $5.48 or 5.48%.

Differences in such rates can be explained in part by the type of customers the various classes of banks tend to serve. Except in Mississippi, the bulk of commercial bank loans are made by member banks. These banks, however, tend to specialize in commercial and industrial loans. Non-member banks, on the other hand, tend to concentrate in making loans to individuals. Since large commercial and industrial concerns tend to be better risks and have better access to alternative sources for a supply of funds, interest charged on such loans tend to be lower than in the case of individuals without such advantages.

The existence of legal interest rates in several of the states is also a factor in understanding interest rate differentials — at least the reported interest rates. As already noted, in Georgia the legal rate is 8 per cent per year. Gorgia's banks also received the highest returns on loans of any banks in the South. In Louisiana, on the other hand, the legal rate is 6 per cent and its banks are amongst those with the lowest reported returns.

Table 5.13

Earnings and Interest Ratios by State and by Class of Bank, 1960°

State	Total	National Banks	State Member Banks	State Banks
Alabama				
Earnings on Government obligations	$3.07	$2.87	$3.40	$3.51
Income on loans	6.26	6.08	6.24	6.91
Service charges	0.31	0.31	0.38	0.31
Interest on time deposits	2.65	2.64	2.70	2.64
Florida				
Earnings on Government obligations	3.10	2.99	3.23	3.29
Income on loans	6.52	6.36	6.28	6.91
Service charges	0.41	0.32	0.41	0.63
Interest on time deposits	2.52	2.50	2.67	2.52
Georgia				
Earnings on Government obligations	3.25	3.18	2.62	3.51
Income on loans	6.61	6.35	6.56	7.22
Service charges	0.39	0.37	0.39	0.43
Interest on time deposits	2.56	2.56	2.38	2.60
Louisiana				
Earnings on Government obligations	3.16	2.92	3.55	3.64
Income on loans	5.97	5.75	6.04	6.53
Service charges	0.27	0.24	0.48	0.30
Interest on time deposits	2.45	2.44	2.27	2.50
Maryland				
Earnings on Government obligations	2.94	2.69	3.75	2.99
Income on loans	5.48	5.09	6.06	5.70
Service charges	0.34	0.21	0.51	0.45
Interest on time deposits	2.43	2.31	2.76	2.47
Mississippi				
Earnings on Government obligations	3.67	3.17	3.56	3.96
Income on loans	5.89	5.88	5.99	5.86
Service charges	0.31	0.37	0.36	0.26
Interest on time deposits	2.56	2.48	2.32	2.65

Table 5.13 (Continued)

Earnings and Interest Ratios by State and by Class of Bank, 1960*

State	Total	National Banks	State Member Banks	State Banks
North Carolina				
Earnings on Government obligations	2.94	2.62	3.10	3.09
Income on loans	5.95	5.30	6.17	6.35
Service charges	0.30	0.30	0.27	0.30
Interest on time deposits	2.33	2.19	2.28	2.42
South Carolina				
Earnings on Government obligations	3.18	2.90	3.42	3.69
Income on loans	6.30	6.19	7.33	6.47
Service charges	0.41	0.44	0.46	0.36
Interest on time deposits	2.17	2.01	2.12	2.35
Tennessee				
Earnings on Government obligations	3.02	2.80	3.30	3.55
Income on loans	5.91	5.64	6.97	6.41
Service charges	0.16	0.18	0.13	0.16
Interest on time deposits	2.71	2.69	3.00	2.70
Virginia				
Earnings on Government obligations	2.86	2.83	2.72	3.04
Income on loans	6.17	5.98	6.48	6.39
Service charges	0.30	0.27	0.30	0.39
Interest on time deposits	2.48	2.47	2.53	2.47
West Virginia				
Earnings on Government obligations	3.04	2.97	3.05	3.18
Income on loans	6.27	6.20	6.28	6.43
Service charges	0.18	0.17	0.17	0.21
Interest on time deposits	2.16	2.24	1.85	2.23

Source: Computed from earnings and interest figures furnished by the Federal Deposit Insurance Corporation and from data found in F.D.I.C. *Report No. 54*, pp. 16-64.

*These figures are computed on the basis of income earned on $100 of United States Government obligations, income per $100 of loans, service charges per $100 of deposit accounts, and interest paid per $100 of time and savings deposits.

APPENDIX

A SURVEY OF SOUTHERN STATE AND NATIONAL BANKING LAWS

Key:

A = State Bank Departments
B = Branch Banking restrictions
C = Capital requirements
D = Maximum rate of interest
E = Maximum loan to any one borrower
F = Reserve requirements
G = Surplus fund requirements
H = Rates of exchange

ALABAMA[1]

A = State banks are controlled by a Superintendent of Banking and a Board of six members appointed by the governor.

B = Branch banking is permitted in counties having 200,000 residents and permitted if the branch was established before 1940.

C = Capital requirements are:

$ 25,000 in cities of less than 3,000
50,000 .... 3,000 to 6.000
100,000 .... 6,000 to 50,000
200,000 .... 50,000 and over

D = The maximum rate of interest is 6 per cent per annum.

E = Any loan to one borrower cannot exceed 20 per cent of aggregate capital.

F = Banks must hold 15 per cent of demand deposits and 5 per cent of time deposits in cash, government bonds, or deposits with other banks to meet the minimum reserve requirements.

G = Alabama requirements that banks hold in a surplus fund an amount equal to 20 per cent of their capital.

H = Banks may charge a rate of exchange no greater than ⅛ of 1 per cent, or a minimum of ten cents per check.

FLORIDA[2]

A = State Banks are controlled by the State Comptroller, who is also the Commissioner of Banking.

B = No branch banking is permitted in Florida.

C = Capital requirements are:

$ 25,000 in cities of less than 5,000
50,000 .... 5,000 to 10,000
100,000 .... 10,000 to 50,000
200,000 .... 50,000 to 200,000
300,000 .... 200,000 and over

D = The maximum rate of interest is 6 per cent per annum.

E = Any loan to one borrower cannot exceed 10 per cent of capital.

F = Banks must hold 20 per cent of aggregate deposits in reserve.

G = Banks are required to hold a surplus fund equal to 20 per cent of capital.

H = Banks can hold only first mortgages and can invest in no corporate stock. Banks may charge a rate of exchange no greater than ¼ of 1 per cent or a minimum of twenty-five cents per check.

---

[1]*The Banking Laws of Alabama*, (Annonated), Reprinted from the Code of Alabama 1940, (Charlottesville, Virginia: The Mitchie Company, 1956), pp. 55-77.

[2]Statutory Revision Department, *Laws of the State of Florida*, Relating to Banks, etc., (Tallahassee, Florida: State of Florida, 1957) pp. 4-40.

GEORGIA[3]

A = State banks are controlled by a Superintendent of Banking appointed by the governor.

B = Branch banking is permitted within any municipal corporation of 80,000 or more, and in areas with a population of less than 80,000, one branch office is permitted per bank.

C = Capital requirements are:
> $25,000 in cities of less than 75,000
> 50,000 in cities of 75,000 and over.

D = The maximum rate of interest is 8 per cent per annum.

E = Any loan to one borrower cannot exceed 20 per cent of aggregate capital.

F = Banks must hold 15 per cent of demand deposits and 5 per cent of time deposits in reserve.

G = Georgia requires that banks hold in a surplus fund an amount equal to 20 per cent of their capital stock.

H = No legal limitation is given for exchange rates in Georgia. (Figures show that in 1960, 67 per cent of Georgia's banks charged exchange rates).

LOUISIANA[4]

A = State banks are controlled by a Banking Commissioner appointed by the governor.

B = Branch banks may be opened within the parent bank's parish if the parent banks has $100,000 in capital. Banks in Allen, Calcasien, Cameron or Jefferson Davis Parishes may have branch banks in any other parish. No bank shall have more than one branch in any parish.

C = Capital requirements are:
> $ 25,000 in cities of less than 3,000
> 50,000_____3,000 to 30,000
> 100,000_____30,000 and over.

D = The maximum rate of interest is 8 per cent.

E = Any loan to one borrower cannot exceed 20 per cent of capital stock.

F = Banks must hold 20 per cent of aggregate deposits in cash or on deposit with other banks, or in U.S. government securities to meet the reserve requirements.

G = Louisiana requires that banks hold in a surplus fund an amount equal to 50 per cent of their capital.

H = Banks may charge a rate of exchange no greater than 1/10 of 1 per cent or a minimum of ten cents per check.

MARYLAND[5]

A = State banks are controlled by a Bank Commissioner appointed by the governor, and by a Banking Board of three, also, appointed by the governor. The Board shall have one member from the Baltimore Clearing House, one from the Associated Mutual Savings Banks of Baltimore, and one of the Maryland State Banker's Association.

B = Capital requirements are:
> $ 25,000 in a city of less than 15,000
> 75,000_____15,000 to 50,000
> 100,000_____50,000 to 150,000
> 500,000_____150,000 and over.

---

[3]State Banking Department, *The Banking Law and the Trust Company Law of the State of Georgia*, (Atlanta, Georgia: State of Georgia, 1960) pp. 3-104.

[4]*Laws of the State of Louisiana*, Related to Banks and Banking, (State of Louisiana, 1952) pp. 1-114.

[5]*Laws*, Related to State Banks, etc., (State of Maryland, 1959) pp. 1-17.

C = The maximum rate of interest is 6 per cent.

D = Any loan to one borrower cannot exceed 10 per cent of capital.

E = Banks must hold 15 per cent of demand deposits and 3 per cent of time deposits in reserve.

F = Maryland requires that banks hold a surplus fund equal to 20 per cent of capital.

H = No legal limitation is given for exchange rates in Maryland. (In 1960, no banks charged exchange in Maryland.)

MISSISSIPPI[6]

A = State banks are controlled by the State Comptroller and Banking Board. The Board is composed of the State Comptroller and four appointed by the governor.

B = Branch banks may be opened in a city of 10,000 or more, in any adjacent county or parent bank's home county; but may not be opened in towns of 3,500 or less having presently only one bank. The parent bank may open no more than 15 branches within a radius of 100 miles. To open a bank, the parent must have $100,000 in capital plus what would be required in the branch bank's city.

C = Capital requirements are:

$25,000 in cities of 6,000 or less.	
35,000	6,000 or 10,000
50,000	10,000 or more.

D = The rate of interest charged shall not exceed that charged by National Banks.

E = Any loan to one borrower cannot exceed 15 per cent of aggregate capital.

F = Banks must hold 15 per cent of demand deposits and 7 per cent of time deposits in reserves if the bank is located in a city of 50,000 or less. In a city of 50,000 or more, banks must hold 25 per cent of demand deposits and 10 per cent of time deposits in reserve.

G = Mississippi requires that banks hold in a surplus fund an amount equal to total capital.

H = Banks may charge a rate of exchange no greater than 1/10 of 1 per cent, or a minimum of ten cents per check.

NORTH CAROLINA[7]

A = State banks are controlled by a Bank Commissioner and by a State Banking Commission composed of ten members. All are appointed by the governor except the Attorney General and the State Treasurer.

B = Branch banks may be opened anywhere provided that the parent bank has capital of an amount equal to that required of unit banks for each office.

C = Capital requirements are:

$ 50,000 in cities of 3,000 or less	
75,000	3,000 to 10,000
100,000	10,000 to 25,000
125,000	25,000 to 50,000
150,000	50,000 and over.

D = The maximum rate of interest is 6 per cent.

E = Any loan to one borrower cannot exceed 20 per cent of capital.

F = Banks must hold 15 per cent of demand deposits and 5 per cent of time deposits in reserve; however, no reserves are required on deposits secured by state or federal bonds.

---

[6]*Mississippi Code*, 1942, (Annotated) Vol. 4A (Atlanta, Georgia: Harrison Company, 1956) pp. 1536-1554

[7]*The Banking Laws of North Carolina*, (Charlottesville, Virginia: The Mitchie Company, 1959) pp. 5-86.

G = North Carolina requires that banks hold in a surplus fund an amount equal to 50 per cent of capital, and be paid in advance of the opening of the bank.

H = Banks may charge a rate of exchange no greater than ⅛ of 1 per cent or a minimum of ten cents per check.

SOUTH CAROLINA [8]

A = Banks are controlled by a State Board of Control, composed of the State Treasurer and four appointed by the governor.

B = Branch banks may be opened anywhere provided that the parent bank has $25,000 in capital in addition to the parent bank's original capital requirements.

C = Capital requirements are:

$ 25,000 in cities of less than 3,000
50,000 .... 3,000 to 10,000
100,000 .... 10,000 or more.

D = The maximum rate of interest is 6 per cent per annum, except on installment loans a rate of 7 per cent may be charged.

E = Any loan to one borrower cannot exceed 15 per cent of capital.

F = Banks must hold 7 per cent of demand deposits and 3 per cent of time deposits in reserve.

G = South Carolina requires that banks hold a surplus fund an amount equal to 25 per cent of capital.

H = No law restricts exchange rates in South Carolina. (In 1960, only 53.4 per cent of the banks in South Carolina remitted at par.)

TENNESSEE[9]

A = Banks in Tennessee are controlled by a Superintendent of Banking appointed by the governor from those recommended by the Tennessee Banker's Association.

B = Branch banks are permitted in only the county of the parent bank.

C = Capital requirements are:

$ 20,000 in cities of 1,000 or less
30,000 .... 1,000 to 2,500
50,000 .... 2,500 to 5,000
75,000 .... 5,000 to 20,000
100,000 .... 20,000 to 50,000
200,000 .... 50,000 and over.

D = The maximum rate of interest is 6 per cent.

E = Any loan to one borrower cannot exceed 15 per cent of capital; 25 per cent of capital is secured by government bonds.

F = Banks must hold 10 per cent of demand deposits and 3 per cent of time deposits in reserve, in cash or demand deposits with other banks.

G = No surplus fund is required by law.

H = Banks may charge a rate of exchange no greater than 1/10 of 1 per cent, or a minimum of ten cents per check.

VIRGINIA[10]

A = State banks are controlled by the State Corporate Commission, Bureau of Banking under the direction of a Commissioner of Banking.

---

[8]*South Carolina Statutes and Regulations,* Relating to Banks, etc. (Charlottesville, Virginia: The Mitchie Company, 1953) pp. 403-528.

[9]*Banking Laws of the State of Tennessee,* (Charlottesville, Virginia: The Mitchie Company, 1952) pp. 44-63.

[10]*Statutes of Virginia,* Relating to Banks, etc., (Charlottesville, Virginia; The Mitchie Company, 1960) pp. 5-47.

B = Branch banks may be opened in the city or county of the parent bank depending on which the parent bank is, and provided the bank has $50,000 in additional capital.
C = Capital requirements are $50,000 minimum up to a city of 25,000 and for every additional 10,000, add $5,000 to the capital requirements.
D = The maximum rate of interest is 6 per cent.
E = Any loan to one borrower cannot exceed 15 per cent of capital.
F = Banks must hold 10 per cent of demand deposits and 3 per cent of time deposits in reserve.
G = Virginia requires that banks hold in a surplus fund an amount equal to 20 per cent of capital.
H = Banks may charge a rate of exchange no greater than ½ of 1 per cent.

WEST VIRGINIA[11]

A = Banks are controlled by a Commissioner of Banking appointed by the governor.
B = Branch banking is forbidden in West Virginia.
C = Capital requirements are:

$ 25,000 in cities of 3,000 or less
50,000 ....3,000 to 6,000
100,000 ....6,000 to 50,000
150,000 ....50,000 or more.

D = The maximum rate of interest is 6 per cent.
E = Any one borrower cannot exceed 10 per cent of capital and surplus.
F = Banks must hold 10 per cent of demand deposits and 5 per cent of time deposits in reserve. 4/5th of the reserves can be in balances due from other banks.
G = West Virginia has no set surplus fund requirements.
H = No law restricts exchange charges in West Virginia. (In 1960, all banks were remitting at par.)

NATIONAL BANKS[12]

A = National Banks are controlled by the Board of Governors of the Federal Reserve System.
B = Branch banking is permitted in states permitting branch banking provided that the parent bank's capital meets the required minimum for each city.
C = Capital requirements are:

$ 50,000 in cities of less than 6,000
100,000................6,000 to 50,000
200,000................50,000 or more

D = The maximum rate of interest is presently 6 per cent per annum.
E = Any loan to one borrower cannot exceed 10 per cent of capital.
F = Banks not in reserve cities must hold a net balance of 7 per cent of demand deposits and 3 per cent of time deposits with the Federal Reserve Bank of its district. Banks in reserve cities and in Central reserve cities must hold 10 per cent of demand deposits and 3 per cent of time deposits with the Federal Reserve Bank of their district.
G = National Banks are required to have a surplus fund equal to 20 per cent of their capital paid in advance to bank opening.
H = No National Bank is permitted to charge an exchange rate.

[11]*The West Virginia Code of 1961*, Vol. 2 (Charlottesville, Virginia: The Mitchie Company, 1961) pp. 640-688.
[12]*The Federal Reserve Act* (Washington, D.C.; The Government Printing Office, 1961) pp. 126-161.

CHAPTER 6

OPERATING RATIOS OF MEMBER BANKS

The bulk of commercial banking in the United States is conducted by member banks of the Federal Reserve System. Consequently, the remainder of this study will concern itself with member banks in the several Federal Reserve Districts. Data on which the analysis rests is obtained from the operating ratios for all member banks. Accordingly, the purpose of this chapter is to discuss these data.

In order to judge the performance of member banks, Federal Reserve Banks conduct annual surveys of operating results of all member banks in their district. Figures for member banks are reduced to a series of percentages or ratios covering earnings, expenses, profits, assets and capital positions. Member banks are then grouped according to deposit size and averages for all banks in each group are worked out. The ratios, printed in a circular by respective Reserve Banks, are sent to each member bank in the district with a transcript of its own ratios.

According to the Federal Reserve Banks, group ratios given in the circular *Operating Ratios of District Member Banks* are not considered goals or standards to be achieved. They are intended to serve as points of departure by member banks, in the analysis of their respective operations. Such information, in effect, is supplementary to a banker's own judgement and knowledge of local conditions.

Table 6.1 presents the nomenclature of operating ratios contained in typical Federal Reserve Surveys. The available material is divided into five parts (1) Summary Ratios; (2) Sources and Disposition of Income; (3) Rates of Return on Securities and Loans; (4) Distribution of Assets; (5) Other Ratios. The bulletin contains information on what are considered to be the more important operating ratios of business including banks. Thus, for example, net revenue reflects the sum total of operations, the judgement of management and the economic circumstances under which a business operated.

Since a bank derives the bulk of its incomes from loans and investments its asset structure is of particular signifi-

Table 6.1

OPERATING RATIOS

(Ratios are expressed in percentages and are arithmetic averages of individual bank percentages)

Deposit Classification in Millions of Dollars

Number of Banks in Deposit Group

SUMMARY RATIOS

Percentage of Total Capital Accounts
1. Net current operating earnings before income taxes.
2. Net Income before related taxes.
3. Net Income
4. Cash Dividends declared.

Percentage of Net Income
5. Cash Dividends declared.
6. Total current operating income.
7. Total current operating expenses.
8. Net current operating earnings before income taxes
9. Net Income.

SOURCES AND DISPOSITION OF INCOME

Percentage of Total Current Operating Income
10. Interest on U.S. Government securities.
11. Interest and dividends on other securities.
12. Income on loans.
13. Service charges on deposit accounts.

Deposit Classification in Millions of Dollars

Number of Banks in Deposit Group

Continued—SOURCES AND DISPOSITION OF INCOME

26. Taxes on net income.
27. Net Income.

RATES OF RETURN ON SECURITIES AND LOANS

Return on Securities
28. Interest on U. S. Government securities.
29. Interest and dividends on other securities.
30. Net recoveries and profits (or losses—) on total securities.

Return on Loans
31. Income on loans.
32. Net recoveries (or losses on Loans).

DISTRIBUTION OF ASSETS

Percentage of Total Assets
33. Cash assets.
34. U. S. Government securities.

14. Other current operating income.
15.   Total Income.
16. Trust department income.
17. Salaries and wages.
18. Officer and employee benefits.
19. Interest on time and savings deposits.
20. Net occupancy expense of bank premises.
21. Other current operating expenses.
22.   Total expenses.
23. Net current operating earnings before income taxes.
24. Net recoveries and profits (or losses—).
25. Net increase (—) or decrease (+) in valuation
       reserves.

35. Other securities.
36. Loans.
37. Real Estate assets.

OTHER RATIOS

In Percentage

38. Total capital accounts to total assets.
39. Total capital accounts to total assets U. S. Govern-
       ment securities and cash assets.
40. Total capital accounts to total deposits.
41. Time (including savings) to total deposits.
42. Interest on time and savings deposits.

cance. The distribution of assets amongst cash, securities, loans, and real estate is shown by the five ratios (numbers 33-37).

The costs of doing business, in the first instance, are summarized by ratios numbered 17-22. Losses and revenue taxes are another of the important factors to be considered by bank management. These items may lead to additions or subtractions from the resources at the disposal of the bank. Thus, recoveries on charged off assets, profits on security sales, or transfers from valuation reserves are but illustrations of possible sources of additions to a bank's resources. Net recoveries and profits (or losses) exclusive of net transfers to or from reserve for bad debts and other valuation reserves are shown in relation to current operating revenue (ratio 24), in relation to the return on securities (ratio 30), and in relation to the return on loans (ratio 32). Taxes on net income (ratio 26) are an important deduction from a bank's revenue and so from the resources at its disposal.

A bank's capital position is summarized by total capital accounts to total assets (ratio 38), total capital accounts to total assets less U.S. Government Securities and cash assets (ratio 39), and total deposits (ratio 40). These are the capital ratios considered important in shedding light on a bank's capital position.

CHAPTER 7

CENTERS AND PERIPHERIES OF ECONOMIC DEVELOPMENT: THE CASE OF THE SIXTH FEDERAL RESERVE DISTRICT

I. HYPOTHESIS

According to the hypothesis developed by T. W. Schultz and others and which is discussed in chapter 1 the product and factor markets will operate more efficiently within a matrix of economic development than they will on the periphery of such matrix.[1] The purpose of this chapter is to examine the empirical consistency of this hypothesis for a part of one factor market, the capital funds market in the 6th Federal District which includes a considerable part of the Southeastern United States. Section II tests the empirical consistency of the hypothesis discussed. Section III presents the conclusions.

II. EMPIRICAL CONSISTENCY OF THE HYPOTHESIS

M. L. Greenhut notes in his location study that August Lösch found support for an implication of the third proportion of Schultz's hypothesis that a significant variation exists between rates charged in the centers of economic development and rates charged on the peripheries of such development in *Federal Reserve Bulletin* statistics on prevailing rates for bank loans and time deposits in Texas cities in 1936. The data indicate that these rates varied with distance from the nearest Reserve Bank city.[2] And John Black writing in 1929 observes that interest rates in all southern and western states were higher than in the more developed areas.[3]

To test the hypothesis that interest rates are higher in

---

[1] This chapter draws extensively from my article "Interest Rates on the Periphery and in the Center of Economic Development," *Southern Economic Journal,* October, 1961, pp. 138-147.

[2] M. L. Greenhut, *Plant Location in Theory and Practice* (Chapel Hill: University of North Carolina Press, 1956), p. 127.

[3] John Black *Production Economics,* (New York: Henry Holt & Co., 1929), p. 199. Quoted in Greenhut *op. cit.,* p. 127.

the periphery than they are in the center of economic development I use earnings on loans to total loans of member banks in the 6th Federal Reserve District. Limiting the analysis to member banks is made necessary by the limitations of data. This should not invalidate the conclusions because these banks do play an important role in the capital funds market of the Southeast. The evidence presented in Table 7.1 shows that although member banks are not as numerous as non-member banks, member banks have on deposit with them the bulk of the bank deposits in the 6th District.

The earning ratio is part of an annual survey of operating rates discussed in Chapter 6 and compiled for the 6th District by the Federal Reserve Bank of Atlanta. For purposes of this chapter the earning ratio of member banks for 1959 is selected. The average ratio of earnings on loans to total loans for each zone represents averages of individual bank ratios, i.e., the averages were not computed from aggregate dollar figures.

Earning ratios are perhaps a better approximation of rates charges by lenders than they are of interest rates paid by borrowers. The differences between lender's rates and borrower's rates is the amount of broker's fees. In the short-run, these two rates will probably move together with the result that earning ratios may serve as a rough indicator for interest rates.

I have selected six urban centers as centers of economic development in the 6th District. These centers are Atlanta, Nashville, Birmingham, New Orleans, Jacksonville, and Miami. The choice of these six centers is dictated by their economic importance in the 6th District. Thus, Atlanta is the location of the head office for the 6th Federal Reserve District while Nashville, Birmingham, New Orleans, and Jacksonville contain branch offices. The choice of Miami, although it does not contain a branch office, can be justified by its dominant economic importance in Southern Florida.

I have selected four geographical zones for each urban center that is assumed to be also a center of economic development. The peripheries of these zones are 50 miles, 100 miles, 150 miles, and 200 miles. The centers ar designated by the first letter of the city and the zones by subscripts 1, 2, 3, and 4.

Table 7.1

Number of Member and Non-Member Banks and their Deposits in the
6th Federal Reserve District, June 10, 1959

($000)

	Member	Non-member	Total	Member	Non-member	Total
Alabama	93	145	238	1,524,633	405,538	1,930,171
Florida	116	170	286	3,258,721	1,352,512	4,611,233
Georgia	64	346	410	1,777,563	863,808	2,641,371
Louisiana	36	76	112	1,568,916	521,690	2,090,606
Mississippi	22	70	92	446,214	315,781	755,995
Tennessee	71	130	201	1,454,375	489,554	1,943,929
Total	402	937	1,339	10,024,422	3,948,883	13,973,305

Source: Research Department, Federal Reserve Bank of Atlanta

Figure 7.1
Development Matrices
in the
Sixth Federal Reserve District

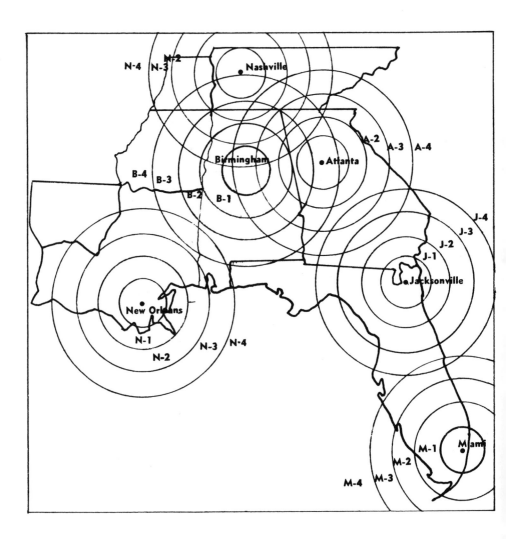

For example, the circle labeled A_1, A_2, A_3, and A_4 represents "A" for Atlanta and the subscripts 1, 2, 3, and 4 the zones. The centers and their zones are represented in figure 7.1.

Since member bank data on individual bank operations are considered confidential, the staff of the Federal Reserve Bank of Atlanta collected and classified earning ratios by size of bank as judged by the size of its deposits and by zone location. Several deposit categories are available but I shall use primarily two. One is up to ten million dollars and the other is ten million dollars and over. The choice of these two size categories is dictated by the availability of data for the several zones and centers of economic development.

The banks are identified by exact location. They are then placed into their respective zones. A bank located in Atlanta is placed into Zone A. When a bank is located, for example, in two or more zones, e.g., A_1 and B_4, it is eliminated from the zone furthest from the city considered as the center of economic development. Moreover, banks are excluded from one zone when they fall within a county through which a line runs but are outside the zone.

Although there are ample economic reasons for the choice of the selected urban centers, the choice of their zones is dictated more by the availability of data than by economic reasons.[4] Fortunately, this is not critically important. What is important is that once the choice of zones is made that it be consistently followed.

A slightly different approach to that adopted in this chapter but more relevant in the economic sense is to take a relatively well developed county as the center of economic development and as the periphery a number of poorer neighboring counties. This approach has much to recommend it. Such an approach would avoid one limitation. And this is that banks included in the centers as well as on the peripheries of economic development are members of the Federal Reserve System. For example, the poorer counties of Georgia are excluded from the analysis since members of the Federal Reserve System are not located in these counties. However, the

---

[4] For a discussion of location theory see Melvin L. Greenhut, *Plant Location in Theory and Practice* (Chapel Hill, N.C.: University of North Carolina Press, 1956).

lack of adequate data on earning ratios of non-member banks excludes the adoption of the above approach. Furthermore, even when a member of the Federal Reserve System is located in one of the poorer counties, the Federal Reserve Bank of Atlanta is bound by the rule of not releasing confidential data for individual banks or for groups of banks when the number is less than three.

Let us now test the empirical validity of the hypothesis discussed in this chapter. Do earning ratios vary from one periphery or zone to another? Do earning ratios vary among the member banks themselves according to deposit size?

In order to answer these questions the technique or two criterion analysis of variance with disproportionate class frequencies is useful. And the method that I shall use, owing to the disproportionate class frequencies, is that of unweighted means. Accordingly, the total variation in data on earning ratios of member banks in the 6th Federal Reserve District is divided into the variation attributable to bank size (row effect), the variation attributable to zone (column effect), and the interaction between bank size and zone.[5]

A summary of the results of the analysis for the several economic development matrices is presented in Table 7.2. In none of the matrices of development presented in the table are variations in member bank earning ratios between zones statistically significant at either the .05 and .01 level. Earning ratios vary significantly between member banks according to their deposit size in four of the seven cases presented in the table. In one of the seven cases, New Orleans and between peripheries NO_1 and NO_3, interaction between bank size and zones is significant. The test results in this case are therefore inconclusive.

The above analysis is focused on selected areas in the 6th District and on several deposit size categories. The overall picture, however, is not substantially altered if the entire District is considered simultaneously. In order to analyze the entire District simultaneously the deposit size category is reduced, owing to available data and in the interests of sim-

---

[5] For details of the analysis of variance with disproportionate class frequencies and the method of unweighted means see W. Allen Wallis, "Lectures on Statistical Inference," given at the University of Chicago during 1949-50.

Table 7.2

Analysis of Variance and Tests of Significance for Atlanta, Birmingham, Nashville, New Orleans, Jacksonville, and Miami Matrices of Economic Development

Matrix [4]	Source of Variation	Sum of Squares	Degrees of Freedom	Mean Square	"F" Value
Atlanta, A_1-A_4	Between Zones	.50	3	.17	1.70
	Between Bank Size	1.86	2	.93	9.30**
	Interaction	.99	6	.17	1.70
	Error	13.89	133	.10	
	Total	17.24	144		
Birmingham, B_2,B_3,B_4	Between Zones	.16	2	.08	1.14
	Between Bank Size[1]	1.34	2	.67	9.57**
	Interaction	.05	4	.01	.14
	Error	8.17	123	.07	
	Total	9.72	131		
Nashville, N_1,N_2,N_4	Between Zones	10.47	2	.06	.50
	Between Bank Size[1]	1.18	2	.59	4.92*
	Interaction	7.11	4	.08	.66
	Error	7.31	61	.12	
	Total	26.07	69		
New Orleans, NO_2,NO_3	Between Zones	.13	1	.13	2.17
	Between Bank Size[2]	.04	1	.04	.67

Table 7.2—Continued

Interaction	.33	1	.33	5.50*
Error	.98	17	.06	
Total	1.48	20		
New Orleans, NO_1, NO_4				
Between Zones	.44	1	.44	1.76
Between Bank Size[3]	1.02	1	1.02	4.08
Interaction	.02	1	.02	.08
Error	6.45	26	.25	
Total	7.93	29		
Jacksonville, J_1, J_4				
Between Zones	.77	3	.26	1.73
Between Bank Size[2]	.31	1	.31	2.07
Interaction	.31	3	.10	.67
Error	7.90	53	.15	
Total	9.29	60		
Miami, M_1, M_2				
Between Zones	0	1	0	0
Between Bank Size[2]	.62	1	.62	6.20*
Interaction	.21	1	.21	2.10
Error	3.39	34	.10	
Total	4.22	37		

*Significant at .05 level.
**Significant at .01 level.
[1] Three categories: Under $5, $5 to $10 and over $10 million.
[2] Two categories: Under $10 and over $10 million.
[3] Two categories: Under $25 and over $25 million.
[4] Owing to the lack of adequate data on groupings by bank size, in some of the economic matrices, Birmingham, Nashville, New Orleans and Miami, not all of the peripheries of zones are used simultaneously in the analysis.

plicity, to two categories. These categories are "up to $10 million and over $10 million." The results of the analysis are summarized in Table 7.3.

Table 7.3

Analysis of Variance and Tests of Significance for All Matrices of Economic Development in the 6th Federal Reserve District

Source of Variation	Sum of Squares	Degrees of Freedom	Mean Square	"F" Value
Between Zones	2.15	17	.13	1.63
Between Bank Size	2.97	1	2.97	37.12*
Interaction	1.73	17	.10	1.25
Error	34.38	431	.08	
Total	41.23	466		

*Significant at .01 level.

To judge from the results presented in Table 7.3, earning ratios do not vary significantly between the various zones. The variations in these ratios between member banks when classified into two deposit categories are highly significant.

Earning ratios thus vary between deposit size categories but not between peripheries and centers of economic development. In so far as earning ratios of member banks are adequate indicators for interest rates, the empirical evidence is inconsistent with the hypothesis that interest rates tend to vary significantly between peripheries and centers of economic development in the 6th District. This suggests that the market for capital funds served by member banks is as "perfect" on the periphery as in the center of a particular industrial urban complex.

These results are, however, consistent with the hypothesis that although interest rates may be higher in less developed areas of the country owing in part to the greatest risks of enterprise there, they also reflect to a considerable degree the importance of the banking structure. It would seem that a closely knit banking structure such as that of the member banks of the Federal Reserve System provides a nation wide market for capital funds rather than many local money markets. Other factors, of course, have also contributed to the narrowing of regional difference in the price of bank credit. The more obvious of these factors are rapid economic growth and industrialization in the South and West, general improvement in methods of communication, the establishment of financial institutions which tend to contribute to credit fluidity, and extension by large banks of their lending activities on a wide scale throughout the country. Coupled with these factors have have been the rapid growth in recent years of deposits in all regions and the expansion of bank reserves and of bank assets that may be converted readily into reserves. This is a tentative conclusion at this point of the analysis. Subsequent chapters will examine the extent to which earnings on loans and investments are related to the degree of economic development in a District.

Although earning ratios do not vary significantly by location of member banks in the 6th District, they do vary significantly by bank size. The evidence presented in Table 7.4 indicates that smaller banks have significantly higher earning ratios than larger banks. These differences in earning ratios seem to reflect differences in the size and type of business customers and the size and composition of their loan portfolios.

Bank practices in the past have played an important role in determining rates charged to customers. For example, there has been a tendency in the recent past for smaller banks throughout the country to charge concerns of a given size somewhat higher rates than did large banks.[6] This does not necessarily mean that one should conduct business only at large banks. And the reason is that, at the same time, the larger banks charge borrowers of similar size on similar loans a higher rate for loans of less than $1,000 than at the smaller banks. This probably reflects the practice at many large banks of making such loans in the personal loan department where rates are usually higher than in departments devoted entirely to business lending.

---

[6] For a discussion of factors influencing interest rates see Richard Youngdahl, "The Structure of Interest Rates on Business Loans at Member Banks," *Federal Reserve Bulletin*, July 1947, pp. 803-819.

Table 7.4

Means of Earning Ratios and Number of Banks by Area and Bank Size

Area and Bank Size (in Millions of Dollars)	Mean	Number of Banks
1) Atlanta:		
a) Under 5	7.49 ⎫ **	66
b) 5 to 10	6.69 ⎬ **	41
c) Over 10	6.56 ⎭ **	38
2) Birmingham		
a) Under 5	7.54 ⎫ **	58
b) 5 to 10	6.95 ⎬ **	41
c) Over 10	6.55 ⎭ **	33
3) Nashville (N_1, N_3, N_4)		
a) Under 5	7.40 ⎫ **	28
b) 5 to 10	6.77 ⎬ **	21
c) Over 10	6.60 ⎭ *	21
4) New Orleans (NO_2, NO_3)		
a) Under 10	6.54 ⎱ †	11
b) Over 10	6.39 ⎰	10
5) New Orleans (NO_1, NO_4)		
a) Under 25	7.10 ⎱ **	18
b) Over 25	6.04 ⎰	12
6) Jacksonville		
a) Under 10	7.08 ⎱ **	25
b) Over 10	6.66 ⎰	36
7) Miami (M_1, M_2)		
a) Under 10	6.96 ⎱ *	8
b) Over 10	6.40 ⎰	30

*Significant at .05 level.
**Significant at .01 level.
†Significant at .30 level.

In gauging the extent of internal and external capital rationing in the 6th District it would be very useful indeed to have more detailed knowledge of member and non-member bank operations. This is particularly true in the area of bank loans to small business. To judge from available information it is the so-called small business which suffers substantially more capital rationing in production (in the use of capital by firms) than larger firms. It would be useful to determine the contribution of existing bank practices to such capital rationing and higher earning ratios at the smaller banks.

A useful start into an examination of banking practices in the 6th District has been made by the Staff of the Federal Reserve Bank of Atlanta. The Staff's studies indicate that present lending practices and policies of banks in the District differ markedly from those of a decade ago. Brandt and Davis report that the large metropolitan banks changed their lending policy more so than other banks in the District, although banks located in small towns changed theirs too.[7] For example, they write that a small businessman who wanted to borrow from a large metropolitan bank in 1956-57 was probably asked to keep on account with that bank a portion of the loan. And bankers that already had such practices insisted that borrowers maintain higher balances than previously. These and other changes such as more collateral and higher standards of credit worthiness to small business which have the effect of raising interest paid by borrowers may be temporary. They occurred in 1956-57 during a period of tight monetary policy. On the other hand these changes in lending policy may be permanent.

Since the problem of adequate small business financing turns on the issue of long-term credit and equity capital, it may well be that we are asking too much of the commercial banking system. Commercial banks are limited in the extent to which they can make loans outside the field of higher grade, shorter term obligations. And the reason for this is the demand nature of their liabilities.

If it may be that some people are asking too much of the commercial banking system in solving the problem of small business financing, others are asking even more of the Federal Reserve System. The Federal Reserve System should properly concern itself directly, it seems to me, with the behavior of the stock of money and not with interest rates or capital requirements of business whether small, medium, or large in size.

---

[7] Harry Brandt and W. M. David, "Small Business, Tight Credit and District Bankers," *Credit Needs of Business Borrowers and Lending Policies and Practices of Commercial Banks in the Southeast* (Atlanta, Ga.: Federal Reserve Bank of Atlanta, 1960), p. 12.

III. CONCLUSION

This chapter has attempted to ascertain the empirical validity of the hypothesis that there exists a significant variation in interest rates between centers and peripheries of economic development. The results of the statistical tests do not support this hypothesis within the 6th Federal Reserve District which incorporates a substantial area in the Southeastern United States. There is not a statistically signficant variation between earning ratios of member banks located in centers and those located in the peripheries of economic development in the 6th Federal Reserve District. A statistically significant variation in earning ratios occurs between member banks when they are classified by deposit size. The smaller banks have significantly higher earning ratios than the larger banks.

In judging the results presented in this paper caution must be exercised. Only data for members of the Federal System have been considered, which, is both an advantage and a disadvantage. It is an advantage because member banks of the Federal Reserve System have on deposit the greater bulk of deposits in the 6th Federal Reserve District. These banks, in terms of total assets, are in fact the keystone to the banking system in the District. It is a disadvantage in that member banks tend to be similar in a great many respects. A broader analysis of the several Federal Reserve Districts is presented in subsequent chapters.

CHAPTER 8

"LIQUIDITY PREFERENCE" — A SOUTHERN BANKING TRADITION?*

I. HYPOTHESIS

The purpose of this chapter is to examine the empirical consistency of the hypothesis that Southern bankers are impeding the region's development because of their conservative predilection which manifests itself in a comparatively high "liquidity preference." For our purposes the South is defined as the 5th and 6th Federal Reserve Districts. Southern bankers are represented by member banks in these two districts during the period 1950-1960.

Section II discusses the hypothesis and its implications. Section III tests the empirical validity of the hypothesis. Section IV discusses a number of implications for Southern development.

II. THE HYPOTHESIS AND ITS IMPLICATIONS

It seems reasonable to postulate that the size of bank assets tends to be geared roughly to many factors including the magnitude of the loan market. The composition of bank assets, however, reflects attitudes of bank officials, including what might be called their "liquidity preference." The Southern banker may prefer the safety and convenience of greater liquidity to the income he will lose through this attitude. Such an attitude, moreover, would also tend to preserve what in Professor Nicholls' terminology is the "Southern Tradition" with its emphasis on agricultural mores. The new "industrial upstarts" would be prevented from upsetting the existing "status quo," if only because Southern bankers allocate and hold a smaller proportion of their assets in the form of loans. These bankers, however, in substituting leisure for profits would be derelict in carrying out the principal function of

* This chapter draws from my contribution in *Essays on Southern Development* (Chapel Hill: University of North Carolina Press, 1964) edited by M. L. Greenhut and W. Tate Whitman.

commercial banking — namely, the "production" of loans. If this hypothesis is correct, then all other things equal, Southern bankers share much of the responsibility for impeding the South's economic development.

Liquidity in a bank and elsewhere may be defined as the possession of those assets, which can be converted into cash easily, quickly and without significant loss. Although technically fully liquid, a bank's cash assets only imperfectly describe its "liquidity preference." Cash, deposits with correspondent banks and Federal Reserve banks, and cash items in the process of collection are its *primary reserves* and represent working balances used in day-to-day operation of the bank. It is thus only to a very limited extent that cash assets *per se* can be counted among its liquid assets. Commercial banking students consider the so-called *secondary reserve* of short-term, readily marketable, high quality assets as the real source of a bank's liquidity. In effect, these secondary reserves represent its planned liquidity in the sense that a bank can control the quantity it holds of such assets.

Very few assets meet banking requirements for secondary reserves. Short maturity, ready marketability and high quality are tests passed by short-term U.S. Government securities. These securities, in fact, constitute the vast preponderance of secondary reserves of the banking system, although other readily marketable short-term securities of prime quality are also included in the secondary reserves of many banks. At times even the loans made to some very high quality borrowers are counted by banks as constituting their secondary reserves.

For purposes of this chapter I shall consider holdings of U.S. Government securities by banks as an indicator, though an imperfect one, of their liquidity preference; cash asset holdings, though important, are not nearly as accurate an indicator of liquidity preference for reasons discussed above. According to the hypothesis to be tested we should observe that Southern bankers hold a comparatively larger proportion of their assets in the form of U.S. Government securities than banks elsewhere in the country. At the same time, we should expect to observe that Southern bankers allocate a comparatively smaller proportion of their total assets to loans.

III. EMPIRICAL CONSISTENCY OF THE HYPOTHESIS

A. Data and Statistical Tests

In order to test the empirical consistency of the hypothesis that Southern bankers have a relatively higher "liquidity preference," Operating Ratios of member banks in the several Federal Reserve Districts are employed. As discussed in Chapter 6, these data are available by deposit classification of member banks for the several operating ratios including "Distribution of Assets" as a percentage of total assets. The asset category consists of cash, U.S. Government securities, other securities, loans, and real estate assets. The several Federal Reserve Districts are presented in Table 8.1.

Table 8.1

Federal Reserve Districts and Bank Cities*

Federal Reserve District	Federal Reserve Bank City
First District	Boston, Mass.
Second District	New York, N. Y.
Third District	Philadelphia, Pa.
Fourth District	Cleveland, Ohio
Fifth District	Richmond, Va.
Sixth District	Atlanta, Ga.
Seventh District	Chicago, Ill.
Eighth District	St. Louis, Mo.
Ninth District	Minneapolis, Minn.
Tenth District	Kansas City, Mo.
Eleventh District	Dallas, Texas
Twelfth District	San Francisco, Calif.

Source: Federal Reserve Bulletin, July 1956, p. 792.

For the eleven year period 1950-1960 availability of comparable data by deposit bank size limited the study to Federal Reserve Districts two through eleven. Member banks in each of these Districts are divided as nearly as possible into five deposit size categories. In millions of dollars, the sizes considered are 0.5 to 1, 1 to 2, 2 to 5, 5 to 10, and 10 to 25. These are designated bank sizes 1 through 5 respectively.

The statistical analysis is in the form of an analysis of variance involving the following four classifications: year, District, bank size, and asset category. This method of analysis appears to be the most appropriate for the purposes of this chapter. The statistical object is to see if the tests of the various possible interactions with the distribution of assets among the asset categories are significantly different from zero. The results are expected to shed light to preference of banks for the several categories of assets.

In order to examine these preferences among Southern bankers tests are made between Districts 5 and 6 and the rest of the country as well as within these two subdivisions of the area studied. These three sets of comparison, which when taken together give a comparison among all the Federal Reserve Districts, are studies separately as well as together when interactions with bank size in addition to asset distribution are computed. The same is also done in computing interactions between District, bank size and asset distribution classifications. In the analysis of variance presented in Table 8.2 the symbols DA, D_1A, D_2A, D_3A represent respectively asset distribution among all Districts, between Districts 5 and 6 as opposed to Districts 2-4 and 7-11, between Districts 5 and 6 and among Districts 2-4 and 7-11.[1]

---

[1] The proportions in the various asset categories varied from low proportions such as 0.001 to proportions close to 0.50. In order to render the analysis of variance more reliable stabilization of the random variation inherent in the data is achieved by transforming all of the observed proportions by means of the sign $\sqrt{p}$ function, where p is an observed proportion. Expressed in radians these transforms are used in the analysis of variance calculations.

The analysis of variance is further complicated by the absence of data on some bank size categories in a number of Districts. The absence consists of 65 sets of data where each set consists of five proportions describing an asset distribution. These missing values are replaced by averages for the year, District, and bank size combinations involved where these average data are computed from the 2,425 transforms of observed proportions which are available. The analysis of variance calculations are carried out using these estimated

Similarly, comparisons of asset distribution among banks are computed for three subcategories of bank sizes as well as all bank size categories. Higher order interactions involving bank size are, however, computed only among all bank size categories. As presented in Table 8.2, BA represents variation in asset distribution among all five bank size categories; B_1A among first three bank sizes; B_2A among last two bank sizes; B_3A between first three bank size and last two bank size categories.

Interaction of time in years and asset distribution is also computed for two breakdowns among the years in the study but higher order interactions involving time are not. In Table 8.2, TA represents variation among all eleven years; T_1A stands for variation attributable to linear progression; T_2A for variation which cannot be accounted for by a linear progression over time.

F-tests are conducted relative to the mean square for the third order DBTA (District, Bank size, Time Asset category) interaction. The tests of significance for computed F-ratios are on the one per cent significance level so as to take into account the possibility of lack of independence or of failure of other assumptions required for the analysis of variance to hold exactly.

B.   Test Results

All of the F-ratios calculated and presented in Table 8.2 except the one for TD_2A (Time, District 5 as opposed to 6, Asset distribution), are significant at the one per cent probability level of significance. It is also clear from the evidence summarized in the table that some of the differences in asset distribution are much greater than others. For example, the

---

values for the categories for which no data are available as well as the transforms of observed proportions. Although such a procedure is biased, it appears to be the best one available for handling these data. As a consequence the total degrees of freedom in the analysis of variance table are reduced from 2,749 to 2,424 to compensate for the use of these estimates in the place of the missing data. And, of course, a corresponding reduction resulted in the error degrees of freedom which are taken to equal 1,115 instead of 1,440.

The proportions obtained in Chapter 8 and 9 by the above complicated procedures do not differ significantly from the simpler method of weighted averages with the number of banks used as weights. And this is in fact the procedure followed in Chapters 10, 12, and 13.

Table 8.2

Analysis of Variance*

Source		Degrees of Freedom		Mean Square	F-Ratio	
TA		40		0.029657	111.49	
	T_1A		4	0.281924		1059.86
	T_2A		36	0.001627		6.12
DA		36		0.048053	180.65	
	D_1A		4	0.045372		170.57
	D_2A		4	0.021801		81.96
	D_3A		28	0.052186		196.19
BA		16		0.039029	146.73	
	B_1A		8	0.035860		134.81
	B_2A		4	0.004935		18.55
	B_3A		4	0.079460		298.72
TDA		360		0.000774	2.91	
	TD_1A		40	0.000629		2.36
	TD_2A		40	0.000250		0.94
	TD_3A		280	0.000870		3.27
TBA		160		0.001003	3.77	
DBA		144		0.003909	14.70	
	D_1BA		16	0.004123		15.50
	D_2BA		16	0.006824		25.65
	D_3BA		112	0.003462		13.02
ERROR—TDBA		1115		0.000266		

*Note:

DA = Variation in asset distribution among all Districts taken together.

D_1A = Variation in asset distribution in Districts 5 and 6 as opposed to Districts 2-4 and 7-11.

D_2A — Variation in asset distribution in Districts 5 as opposed to District 6.

D_3A = Variation in asset distribution among Districts 2-4 and 7-11.

BA = Variation in asset distribution among all five bank size categories.

B_1A = Variation in asset distribution among first three bank sizes.

B_2A = Variation in asset distribution among last two bank sizes.

B_3A = Variation in asset distribution between first three and last two bank sizes.

TA = Variation in asset distribution among all eleven years of study.

T_1A = Portion of variation attributable to a linear progression over the time of study.

T_2A = Variation in asset distribution which cannot be accounted for by linear progression over time.

mean square for T_1A is 0.281924 while that for T_2A is only 0.001627. This indicates that the changes in asset distributions are mostly linear in pattern over the time period under study even though this linear pattern varies among the asset categories. Such a result is of course expected. If the proportion invested in one asset category increased linearly over the period, a similar decline would be expected in other asset categories.

Table 8.3

Average Percentage Distribution of Assets by Year 1950-60 for
Federal Reserve Districts 2-11 and Bank Sizes 1-5

Year	Asset Categories				
	Government Securities	Other Securities	Loans	Cash	Real Estate
1950	39.6	7.2	29.1	22.6	0.71
1951	37.2	7.3	30.2	23.9	0.72
1952	36.1	7.3	30.8	24.3	0.74
1953	36.0	7.4	31.9	23.2	0.79
1954	35.0	7.5	33.0	23.0	0.80
1955	34.8	7.8	34.0	21.8	0.85
1956	33.6	8.1	35.5	21.1	0.91
1957	33.5	8.3	35.5	21.1	0.97
1958	32.1	8.9	36.6	20.7	1.02
1959	32.1	9.1	37.3	19.8	1.04
1960	31.2	8.8	38.6	19.6	1.09

Regarding the relationship between time and asset distribution the evidence summarized in Table 8.3 is helpful. Average percentages of assets for all Districts and bank sizes are listed by year for each asset category. These averages are computed by calculating arithmetic means on the transformed scale used in the analysis of variance with the estimated missing values included in the computations. These means are then transformed back to the percentage scale to give the averages summarized in Table 8.3.

The evidence contained in the table suggests a steady decline over the eleven year period 1950-1960 in the average proportion of bank assets invested in Government securities. Except for a drop in 1960 relative to 1959 and 1958 there is an upward trend in the proportion of assets invested in other securities. The pattern for cash assets is upward until after 1952 and then is generally downward. The evidence suggests, on the other hand, a steady upward trend in the percentage assets invested in loans and real estate. To judge from these data for the period 1950-60, member banks in Districts 2-11 shifted away from such liquid assets as cash and government securities to loans and real estate assets which are relatively less liquid.

Analysis of variance presented in Table 8.2 shows that the mean square and resulting F-ratio for DA (District, Asset distribution) is very large, indicating a highly significant difference in asset distribution among the several Districts tested. As to the various Districts, D_1A and D_3A have similar mean squares while the mean square for D_2 is smaller though highly significant.

The large mean squares for DA, D_1A D_2A, and D_3A indicate that the asset distributions among Federal Reserve Districts differ from each other by a highly significant amount regardless of whether the comparison is made among Districts 2-11, among Districts 2-4 and 7-11, between Districts 5 and 6 or between Districts 2-4 and 7-11 taken together and Districts 5 and 6 taken together. The evidence thus indicates that every District in the country differs in the asset distribution of its banks.

In order to examine more closely the differences in asset distribution among the several Districts, the average percentage distribution of assets for each District is computed and presented in Table 8.4. The averages are taken over all years and bank size categories and computed in the same manner as those in Table 8.3. Estimates presented in table 8.4 indicate that-member banks in Districts 5 (Richmond), 6 (Atlanta) and 11 (Dallas) invested a smaller proportion of their assets in Government and "other securities" than did member banks in other Districts. Moreover, member banks

Table 8.4

Average Percentage Distribution of Assets by Federal Reserve
Districts 2-11 for Years 1950-60 and Bank Sizes 1-5

Federal Reserve District	Asset Categories				
	Government Securities	Other Securities	Loans	Cash	Real Estate
2	35.2	9.1	35.3	19.3	0.98
3	35.4	8.8	36.6	17.6	1.02
4	35.9	8.4	35.6	18.8	0.88
5	33.9	7.0	35.9	22.1	1.18
6	32.2	7.3	32.8	25.7	1.03
7	38.2	7.7	31.8	20.5	0.72
8	37.6	7.7	30.6	22.8	0.70
9	36.7	8.4	33.6	19.6	0.76
10	33.8	7.6	33.0	24.4	0.56
11	28.3	7.7	33.1	29.3	0.98

in Districts 5 and 6 invested a higher proportion of their assets in real estate than did member banks in other Districts.

Analysis of variance for differences among bank sizes indicates that asset distribution differs significantly at the one per cent probability level among the five bank size categories considered. Moreover, since the mean squares for B_3A and B_1A are much larger than the mean square for B_2A, the difference in asset distribution for bank sizes 1 through 3 as opposed to bank size categories 4 and 5 and the differences among the asset categories within bank sizes 1-3 were greater than the differences between the asset distributions for bank sizes 4 and 5. Indeed, the B_2A mean square is much smaller than all the other mean squares for first order interactions, indicating similar asset distributions for bank sizes 4 and 5. Moreover, the mean square obtained for B_3A is larger than any obtained when the interactions of Districts with asset distribution are compared so that bank size seems to be somewhat more important as a determinant of asset distribution than does location.

The average percentage distribution of assets by bank size is presented in Table 8.5. These averages include data on all Districts throughout the eleven year period of study. They are computed in the same manner as those presented in Tables 8.3 and 8.4. Data in Table 8.5 indicate that the larger the bank size, the greater the concentration of assets in real estate and the smaller the proportion of cash assets. There is also a trend throughout the first four bank sizes for the proportion of assets in "other securities" to go up and in loans to go down as bank size increases.

Table 8.5

Average Percentage Distribution of Assets by Bank Size for Federal Reserve Districts 2-11 and for Years 1950-1960

Bank Size Category	Asset Categories				
	Government Securities	Other Securities	Loans	Cash	Real Estate
1 = small	32.9	6.0	35.1	24.1	0.74
2	35.1	6.8	33.8	23.0	0.73
3	35.2	8.7	33.5	21.1	0.86
4	35.2	9.6	32.8	20.9	0.95
5 = large	34.8	9.0	33.9	20.5	1.11

Bank Size Category:
    1 = $0.5 to $ 1 million in deposits;
    2 = $ 1 to $ 2 million in deposits;
    3 = $ 2 to $ 5 million in deposits;
    4 = $ 5 to $10 million in deposits;
    5 = $ 10 to $25 million in deposits.

Finally, the mean squares for the TDA, TBA, and DBA second order interactions, although significantly greater than the mean square for the third order interaction TDBA which is used as an error term, are much smaller in general than the first order interactions. These higher order interactions, therefore, do not seem nearly as important for the understanding of differences in asset distribution as the interactions with time, location and bank size, taken separately, with the distribution of assets. Location and bank size interact more in their effect on asset distribution than location and time or bank size and time since the mean square for DBA is quite a bit larger than those for TDA or TBA. This is also true for such division of TDA and BDA into interactions involving D_1, D_2 and D_3.

IV. IMPLICATIONS FOR SOUTHERN DEVELOPMENT

Results summarized in this chapter and their apparent inconsistency with the hypothesis that Southern bankers tend to have a higher "liquidity preference" than bankers elsewhere in the country have several implications for Southern development. First, these results indicate that insofar as member banks in the South are concerned they do not appear to be derelict in performing commercial banking's principal function which is the production of loans. In fact, their performance on this score appears to be somewhat better than that of member banks in many other Districts in the country.

Second, the comparatively smaller proportion of their assets held in U. S. Government securities indicates that member banks in the South are not serving as a vehicle for the transfer of resources out of the region. This is because investment in U.S. Government securities is made on a national market and thus, in the first instance, tends to draw resources out of a region. It is, of course, true that loans can also be made on the national market but the majority of loans are on balance made in local market areas.

Third, the evidence suggests that Southern bankers tend to be less "conservative" in their financial outlook than many of their colleagues elsewhere. We should, accordingly, expect to see them actively promoting economic development in the South. The Southern banker apparently has little desire to stop the wheels of progress for the sake of a mystical tradition.

Although suggestive, the results reported in this chapter are by no means conclusive. The reason for not accepting these results as conclusive will become more apparent in Chapter 11. At this point it is sufficient to mention one limitation that should be kept carefully in mind. Non-member banks are not considered in the analysis.

CHAPTER 9

RATES OF EARNINGS ON SECURITIES AND LOANS

I. HYPOTHESIS

In Chapter 7 it is indicated that earnings on loans do not differ significantly among member banks by their location in centers and peripheries of economic development in the 6th Federal Reserve District. We should not expect to observe a similar phenomena for all Districts considered simultaneously owing to the local nature of the market for loans. The securities market on the other hand, tends to be nation-wide in scope. Accordingly, we should expect to observe that significant differences exist in the rates of earnings on loans but not in the rates for securities among the several Federal Reserve Districts. It is the purpose of this chapter to examine the empirical consistency of this hypothesis. Section II discusses the empirical validity of the hypothesis. Section III presents the conclusion.

II. EMPIRICAL CONSISTENCY OF THE HYPOTHESIS

A. Data and Tests

Data for rates of earnings of securities and loans are obtained from Operating Ratios of Member Banks discussed in Chapter 6. A discussion of the tests performed on these data need not be repeated here since they are identical to those discussed and used in examining the "liquidity preference" of Southern bankers in Chapter 8.

For the period 1950-60 member banks in Districts two through eleven are divided, as in Chapter 8, into five deposit size categories and designated into bank sizes 1 through 5. The rates of earnings on three types of assets are considered in the analysis: Government securities, other securities, and loans. A four-fold classification is used in the analysis of variance: Year, District, bank size, and rate of earnings.

In order to examine the rates of earnings on government securities, "other securities" and loans among Southern member banks tests are made between Districts 5 and 6 and the rest of the country as well as within these two subdivisions of the South. These three sets of comparisons, which when taken together give a comparison among all the Federal Reserve Districts considered, are studied separately as well as together when interactions with bank size in addition to the three rates of earnings are computed. The same is also done in computing interactions between District, bank size and rates of earnings categories. In the analysis of variance presented in Table 9.1 the symbols DR, D, R, D_2R, and D_3R represent respectively rates of earnings categories among all Districts, between Districts 5 and 6 as opposed to Districts 2-5 and 7-11, between Districts 5 and 6 and among Districts 2-4 and 7-11.

Comparisons of rates of earnings among banks for three sub-categories of bank sizes are made as well as all bank size

Table 9.1

Analysis of Variance*

Source		Degrees of Freedom		Mean Square	F-Ratio	
TR		20		0.001401	63.7	
	T_1R		2	0.001275		58.0
	T_2R		18	0.000140		6.4
DR		18		0.001572	71.5	
	D_1R		2	0.001444		65.6
	D_2R		2	0.001523		69.2
	D_3R		14	0.001597		72.6
BR		8		0.002304	104.7	
	B_1R		4	0.002088		94.9
	B_2R		2	0.000216		9.8
	B_3R		2	0.004825		219.3
TDR		180		0.000048	2.2	
TBR		80		0.000028	1.3	
DBR		72		0.000150	6.8	
ERROR = TDBR		522		0.000022		

*Note:
Every F-statistic except the one for TBR is significant at the one per cent probability level. The F-statistic for TBR is not significant at either the one or five per cent probability level.

categories. Higher order interactions involving bank size are computed only among all bank size categories. As summarized in Table 9-1, BR represents variation in rates of earnings among all five bank size categories; B_1R among last two bank sizes; B_3R between first three bank size and last two bank size categories.

Interaction of time in years and rates of earnings is computed for two breakdowns among the years 1950-60 but higher order interactions involving time are not. TR in Table 9.1 represents variation among all eleven years; TR represents variation attributable to a linear regression; T_2R stands for variation which cannot be accounted for by a linear regression over time.

F — tests are conducted relative to the mean square for the third order DBTR (District, Bank size, Time, Return category) interaction. The tests of significance for computed F-ratios are on the one per cent level of significance in order to take into account the possibility of lack of independence or of failure of other assumptions required for the analysis of variance to hold exactly.

B.   Test Results and Their Implications

An examination of the evidence summarized in Table 9.1 indicates that all of the F-tests are significant on the one per cent probability level except the one for TBR which is significant neither at the one nor the five per cent probability level. The evidence thus suggests significant differences in the rates of return (or earnings) on securities and loans. Some of these differences, however, are greater than others. For example, the mean square for T_3R is 0.001275 while that for T_2R is 0.000140 indicating that changes in rates of return are linear in pattern over the period 1950-60 even though the linear pattern varies somewhat among rates of return for the three assets.

A clearer picture of the relationship between time and rates of return is provided by the evidence summarized in Table 9.2. The average rates of return for all districts and bank sizes are listed by year for each of the three assets considered. These averages are computed by calculating arith-

Table 9.2

Average Percentage Distribution of Rates of Return on Securities and Loans
by Year from 1950-60 for Federal Reserve Districts 2-11 and Bank Sizes 1-5

Year	Rate of Return Categories		
	U.S. Government Securities	Other Securities	Loans
1950	1.8	2.6	5.7
1951	1.9	2.6	5.8
1952	2.0	2.6	5.9
1953	2.1	2.6	5.9
1954	2.1	2.6	5.9
1955	2.2	2.6	6.0
1956	2.5	2.6	6.0
1957	2.6	2.7	6.3
1958	2.6	2.9	6.3
1959	2.9	2.9	6.4
1960	3.2	3.2	6.6

metic means on the transformed scale used in the analysis
of variances and estimates of missing values are included in
the calculations. The means are then transferred back to the
percentage scale to give the averages summarized in Table
9.2. The outstanding feature of these data is the upward drift
in all three rates of return over the period. This upward drift
appears to be more pronounced in the cases of earnings on
U.S. Government securities and loans. It is only since 1957,
however, that the upward drift in the category "other securities" becomes pronounced.

Consider again the analysis of variance presented in
Table 9.1. The size of the mean square and resultant F-ratio
for DR indicates a significant difference in the rates of return
among the Federal Reserve Districts. Moreover, D_2R and
D_3R leave similar mean square while the mean square for
D_1R is smaller though significant. D_1R contrasts the rates
of return in Districts 5 and 6 taken together with the rates
of return in all other Districts considered. D_2R is concerned

with the differences in rates of return for Federal Reserve Districts 5 and 6 which contain the bulk of the Southern States. D_3R measures the differences in the rates of return among the other Districts. The size of the mean squares for DR, D_1R, D_2R, and D_3R indicate that the rates of return among the Federal Reserve Districts differ from each other by a significant amount regardless of whether the comparison is made among District 2-11, among Districts 2-4 and 7-11, between Districts 5 and 6, or between Districts 5 and 6 taken together.

Table   9.3

Average Percentage Distribution of Rates of Return on Securities and Loans by Federal Reserve Districts 2-11 for Years 1950-1960 and Bank Sizes 1-5

Federal Reserve District	Rate of Return Categories		
	Government Securities	Other Securities	Loan
2	2.3	2.5	5.8
3	2.4	2.9	5.7
4	2.3	2.7	5.6
5	2.4	2.9	6.1
6	2.4	2.9	6.8
7	2.2	2.5	5.7
8	2.3	2.7	5.9
9	2.4	2.6	5.9
10	2.3	2.7	6.4
11	2.4	2.9	7.0

In order to examine the differences in rates of return among the Federal Reserve Districts more closely, the average rate of return for each of three types of assets is presented in Table 9.3. The estimates are taken over the entire period 1950-60 and for all bank sizes and computed in the same manner as those in Table 9.2. The evidence summarized in Table 9.3 indicates that rates of return from loans to member banks in Districts 5, 6 and 11 are higher than those to member banks in other Districts. As indicated in Chapter 8 member banks in these three Districts also invest less money in securities than banks elsewhere. This is what we should expect to observe if banks are playing their role in the allocation of resources. The national market in U.S. government securities is clearly suggested in the similarity of the rates of return for these securities in the several Districts. The rates of return in the category "other securities" are also somewhat higher for member banks in Districts 5, 6 and 11 (though this appears true also for District 3) than for the other Districts.

The analysis of variance for differences among bank sizes shows that rates of return differ significantly at the one per cent probability level among the five bank size categories considered. Also, since the mean squares for B_3R and B_1R are much larger than the mean square for B_2R, the differences in rates of return to bank sizes 1 through 3 as opposed to bank size categories 4 and 5 and the differences among the rates of return within bank sizes 1-3 are greater than the differences between the rates of return for bank sizes 4 and 5. In fact, the B_2R mean square is much smaller than all other mean squares for first order interactions, indicating similar rates of return for bank sizes 4 and 5. Moreover, the mean square obtained for B_3R is more than those obtained for the interactions of districts with rates of return so that bank size, at least whether or not a bank has total deposits less than or greater than five million dollars, seems to be somewhat more important as a determinant of rates of return than does location.

The average rate of return by bank size is presented in Table 9.4. The figures include data on all districts throughout the time period studied. These estimates are computed in the same manner as those presented in Tables 9-2 and 9.3 The evidence summarized in Table 9.4 indicates that the smaller the bank size the larger are the rates of return realized on loans and "other securities".

Finally, the mean squares for TDR, TBR, and DBR second order interactions, although greater than the mean square for the third order interaction TDBR which is used as an error term, are smaller in general than the first order

Table 9.4

Average Percentage Distribution of Rates of Return on Securities and Loans by Bank Size for Federal Reserve Districts 2-11 and For Years 1950-1960

Bank Size Category	Asset Categories		
	Government Securities	Other Securities	Loans
1 = small	2.4	3.2	6.5
2	2.4	3.0	6.2
3	2.4	2.6	6.0
4	2.3	2.4	5.9
5 = large	2.2	2.4	5.7

interactions. These higher order interactions, therefore, do not seem nearly as important for the understanding of differences in rates of return as do the interactions with time, location and bank size, taken separately, with the rates of return. Location and bank size interact more in their effect on the rates of return than does location and time or bank size and time.

III.   CONCLUSION

At least three important conclusions are suggested by the analysis and evidence presented in this chapter. First, differences in rates of earnings exist among district, bank size categories, and among the three asset categories U.S. Government securities, other securities, and loans. Southern member banks in the 5th and 6th Districts registered higher rates of earning on loans than all other Districts except Districts 10 (Kansas City) and 11 (Dallas). To judge from the evidence on the asset distribution of banks, these Districts also tend to be among the leaders in the proportion of their assets held in loans. Such evidence is consistent with the role played by banks in allocating resources.

Second, Southern banking is an integral part of the American financial scene. It shares with banking elsewhere in the country the characteristic of participating in the nation-wide U.S. Government securities market. The similarity of the rates of earning on such securities is testimony to such participation. Rates of earnings on "other securities" also tend to be similar so that nation-wide participation is not limited only to the U.S. Government securities market.

Third, the evidence clearly suggested the local nature of the market for loans. And, it is the difference in the rates of earnings on loans that account for most of the differences among banks. This is true whether banks are classified by deposit size or Federal Reserve District.

CHAPTER 10

PROFITABILITY OF MEMBER BANKING

I. HYPOTHESIS

An implication of T. W. Schultz's hypothesis discussed
in Chapter 1 is that banks located in relatively underdeveloped
regions tend to be more profitable than those located in
the more developed regions owing to the relative scarcity
of the bundle of resources that they represent. Accordingly,
we should expect to observe that an inverse relationship
exists between bank profitability and the degree of economic
development in the District as measured by per capita personal income.

Profitability of banking can be measured in three ways.[1]
First, by returns on bank capital; second, by returns on total
assets; third, by returns to loans and investments. These
three measures shed light on diverse aspects of bank operations. Returns on capital measure profitability from the standpoint of entry or exit. Returns on total assets reflect the basic
earning power of an organization. Returns on loans and investments suggest the net markup on bank output.

The purpose of this chapter is to test the empirical consistency of our hypotheses against all three measures of bank
profitability. Section II examines returns by bank size. Section III discusses returns by Federal Reserve District. Section IV analyzes bank returns over the period 1950-60. Section V presents the conclusions.

II. RETURNS BY BANK SIZE

Consider the returns to capital by bank size. Because of
the higher degree of sophistication that tends to prevail in
larger banks and which presumably leads them to make maximum use of their opportunities, we should expect to observe
that the returns to capital increase by bank size.

---

[1] David A. Alhadeff, *Monopoly and Competition in Banking* (Berkeley:
University of California Press, 1954) p. 173.

Table 10.1 summarizes some relevant data useful in gauging the performance of banks by size. The evidence indicates that our expectation is fulfilled. Returns to capital do in fact increase by bank size. This is true for net current earnings and profits before taxes. It is also true for net profits and cash dividends declared.

To judge from these data the larger the bank the more closely is it tied to the capital funds market and thus the less likely are its capital needs to pose special problems for the economy. Indeed, on the economic criteria that resources should be allocated into areas where the highest returns can be obtained then, all other things equal, the larger banks are more preferable than the smaller organizations. Broader public participation in the larger banks is suggested by the tendency on the part of these banks to distribute percentage-wise more of their net profits.

As in other industries, however, it may also be that smaller commercial banks experience greater difficulty in floating their securities on the open market and so must depend more on retained earnings than the larger organizations as a source of additional capital. In effect, capital market imperfections may force the smaller banks into a situation where they leave little choice but to resort to retained earnings if they are to obtain additional capital.

On the other hand, the profitability of the larger banks is not unambiguous when returns on total assets are considered. To judge from the evidence summarized in Table 10.2 little relationship appears to exist between bank size and returns on earnings on bank assets.

The apparent inverse relationship that exists between "net profits after taxes" and bank size can be attributed to the nature of the tax system rather than to bank size as such. Consider, for example, the figures summarizing "net current earnings before income taxes." The estimate for the smallest bank with deposits up to $2 million is the same as for the penultimate bank with deposits of $25 million and over. Insofar as total earnings are concerned, the best performance is obtained by banks in the deposit size category $10-25 million. And indeed the poorest performance on this score is given by the largest organizations.

Table 10.1

Average Percentage Distribution of Earnings on Total Capital
Accounts. By Bank Size for Federal Reserve Districts
2-11 and for Years 1960-60

Bank Size Category	Net Current Earnings Before Income Taxes	Percentage of Total Capital Accounts			
		Profits Made Before Income Taxes	Net Profits	Cash Dividends Declared	Percentage of Net Profits Distributed
Group I	12.58	11.12	8.45	2.84	33.60
Group II	14.26	12.35	8.78	3.03	34.51
Group III	15.81	13.26	8.79	3.10	35.26
Group IV	16.73	14.18	8.85	3.19	36.04
Group V	17.97	15.38	9.06	3.40	37.52

Group I   = Banks with deposits up to $2 million.
Group II = Banks with deposits $2 million - $5 million.
Group III = Banks with deposits $5 million - $10 million.
Group IV = Banks with deposits $10 million - $25 million.
Group V   = Banks with deposits $25 million and over.

Table 10.2

Average Percentage Distribution of Earnings on Total Assets by Bank Size
for Federal Reserve Districts 2-11 and for Years 1950-1960

Bank Size Category*	Percentage of Total Assets		
	Total Earnings	Net Current Earnings Before Income Taxes	Net Profits After Taxes
I	3.44	1.17	0.78
II	3.37	1.15	0.71
III	3.43	1.15	0.64
IV	3.47	1.15	0.61
V	3.34	1.17	0.59

* I Deposits = 0-$2 Million
  II Deposits = 2-5 Million
 III Deposits = 5-10 Million
 IV Deposits = 10-25 Million
  V Deposits = 25 Million and Over

These results appear in contrast to those obtained by
the preceding measure of bank profitability which suggested
that returns to capital and size of bank are positively cor-
related. The explanation is simple enough. The two measures
of profitability differ conceptually. Returns to total assets
measures the fundamental earning capacity of the organization. Furthermore, it removes the influence of the capital-
deposit ratio implicit in the returns to capital measure which
is largely a function of size and banking organization rather
than individual performance.[2]

The discussion and results on earnings on loans and
securities presented in Chapter 9 suggests that an inverse
relationship exists between bank size and returns on loans
and securities. This relationship is more pronounced in the
case of returns to loans than for securities. In part, the explanation is that loan size, loan mix, and market structures
in which the various size banks operate differs. The smaller
banks tend to obtain higher returns on loans because of the

---

[2] *Ibid.*, p. 191.

nature of the loans that they make. They do not concentrate as much as the larger banks in strictly business loans. Such loans tend to be larger and less risky and hence the smaller return to the larger banks. And undoubtedly the problem is to some extent compounded by elements of monopoly in the loan market in which small banks operate.

III. RETURNS TO MEMBER BANKS BY FEDERAL RESERVE DISTRICTS

We should expect to observe that an inverse relationship exists between returns to member banks and District per capita personal income. In regions which are relatively underdeveloped economically returns to the type of resources embodied in banking tend to be higher owing to the relative scarcity of these resources. All other things equal, these higher returns act as a magnet to attract such resources and so lower their returns. In effect, these returns are but one manifestation of the price system's operation.

Tables 10.3, 10.4 and 10.5 in addition to Table 9.3 summarize the relevant evidence on returns to member banks. The evidence is consistent with our expectation of returns in bank capital. The Spearman rank correlation coefficient $\curvearrowright$, which is a non-parametric test of association between net profits on bank capital and per capita income is —.591 and significant at .05 level. The sign of the coefficient is negative indicating an inverse relationship between income and returns.

Member banks in the underdeveloped Districts also declare relatively larger dividends suggesting thereby that they are in close contact with the market for capital funds. Thus, the Spearman rank correlation coefficient between dividends declared and per capita income is —.569 which is significant at the .05 level.

It would seem that this evidence is also consistent with the existence of more "sophisticated" investors in the developed regions for whom, presumably, smaller dividends are no bar to investment. Thus, for example, there is a tendency on the part of banks located in the more developed regions to pay out a smaller percentage of their net profits in dividends.

Table 10.3

Average Per Capita Personal Income in Dollars for Federal Reserve
Districts 2-11, 1950-60

Average Per Capita Income	District									
	2	3	4	5	6	7	8	9	10	11
	2319	1981	2061	1544	1332	2059	1506	1675	1717	2165

Source: Same as Table 3.1.

The rank correlation coefficient between percentage of net profits distributed and per capita income is —.177. The relationship, however, is not particularly important since the correlation coefficient is not statistically significant at either the .01 or .05 levels.

On the other hand, for all Districts considered in the analysis, the rank correlation coefficient between net profits and dividends is +.980 which is significant at the .01 level. There is thus a very strong relationship between the size of net profits and the amount of dividends declared. In effect, the higher a bank's profits the more likely it is to declare a larger dividend. And the converse is true. All of this suggests that perhaps too much has been made by some people of the willingness on the part of sophisticated investors to take their returns in something other than cash. It is not very likely that such investors will continually prefer less profitable banks.

Consider now returns to total assets by Federal Reserve District. To judge from the Spearman rank correlation coefficient the evidence with our hypothesis. There does exist an inverse relationship between returns to member bank assets and per capita personal income. For District income and total returns of assets the correlation coefficient is +.321. This does not indicate a very strong relationship since the coefficient is not significant at the .05 level. On the other hand, for income and net current earnings before taxes the coefficient is —.681 and significant at the .05 level indicating a strong inverse relationship which is consistent with our expectation. This conclusion is reinforced by a rank correlation co-

Table 10.4

Average Percentage Distribution of Earnings on Total Capital Accounts by Federal Reserve
Districts 2-11 for Years 1950-1960 and Bank Sizes 1-5

Federal Reserve District	Net Current Earnings Before Income Taxes	Percentage of Total Capital Accounts			Percentage of Net Profits Distributed
		Profits Made Before Income Taxes	Net Profits	Cash Dividends Declared	
2	12.46	10.42	7.16	2.69	37.56
3	11.42	9.91	6.92	2.62	37.86
4	13.32	11.62	7.90	2.73	34.55
5	14.20	12.75	8.35	3.01	36.04
6	16.12	13.72	9.23	3.06	33.15
7	15.45	13.27	9.16	2.83	30.89
8	15.05	13.02	9.07	2.98	32.85
9	17.36	15.18	10.04	3.73	37.15
10	16.40	14.13	9.65	3.45	35.75
11	16.03	12.90	9.00	3.54	39.33

Table 10.5

Average Percentage Distribution of Earnings on Total Assets for Districts 2-11 for Years 1950-60 and Bank Sizes 1-5

Federal Reserve District	Percentage of Total Assets		
	Total Earnings	Net Current Earnings Before Income Taxes	Net Profits After Taxes
2	3.48	1.01	0.58
3	3.38	1.11	0.68
4	3.30	1.16	0.67
5	3.48	1.18	0.70
6	3.61	1.18	0.68
7	3.20	1.06	0.64
8	3.18	1.67	0.71
9	3.63	1.21	0.71
10	3.47	1.28	0.76
11	3.48	1.22	0.70

efficient of —.591 between District income and net current earnings after taxes which is significant at the .05 level.

According to the evidence summarized in Table 9.3 returns on government securities do not differ significantly amongst the several Districts. On the other hand, the returns on "other securities" and incomes are inversely related. The rank correlation coefficient is +.565 and significant at .05 level. So, too are the returns on loans and District incomes inversely related. Thus, the rank correlation coefficient between returns on loans and income is —.759 which is significant at the 0.1 level. Again this evidence is consistent with our hypothesis.

IV. PROFITABILITY OF MEMBER BANKING, 1950-60

To judge from the evidence summarized in Table 10.6 returns to member bank capital remained relatively stable over the period 1950-60. This is confirmed by a simple test

Table 10.6

Average Percentage Distribution of Earnings on Total Capital Accounts by Year from 1950-1960 for Federal Reserve Districts 2-11 and Bank Sizes 1-5

| Year | Percentage of Total Capital Accounts | | | | Percentage of Net Profits Distributed |
	Net Current Earnings Before Income Taxes	Profits Made Before Income Taxes	Net Profits	Cash Dividends Declared	
1950	14.86	13.17	9.83	3.04	30.92
1951	14.67	12.79	9.19	3.02	32.86
1952	15.25	13.25	8.87	3.00	33.82
1953	15.06	13.01	8.42	2.93	34.79
1954	14.38	14.12	9.53	3.02	31.68
1955	14.84	12.27	7.88	3.03	38.45
1956	15.24	11.52	7.70	3.04	39.48
1957	14.65	11.75	7.92	3.09	39.01
1958	13.37	12.97	8.85	3.08	34.80
1959	15.10	11.41	7.77	3.10	39.89
1960	15.12	13.02	9.23	3.16	34.23

for the predominance of upward or downward movements.[3] The test amounts to counting the number of plus and minus signs. If neither direction of movement predominates, the two signs should be equally numerous, except for chance variations.[4]

The value of the standard normal variable K for cash dividends is 1.50 which is not significant at the .05 level indicating that no evidence for a trend exists. The same is true for net profits and percentage of net profits distributed. For profits before taxes and net current earnings K is .5 which is not significant at the .05 level indicating again that no evidence for a trend is provided by our simple test. It should be noted, however, that the upward movements may be on the average larger, or smaller than the downward movements. Such a trend would not be detected by this test.

Some indication as to the course of returns to bank capital in recession years is provided by the evidence in Table 10.6. In the two recession years 1954 and 1958 net current earnings and percentage of net profits distributed declined. Profits before and after taxes and cash dividends declared on the other hand increased. This is what we should expect. When interest rates decline as they tend to do in recession periods, the price of securities rises. Banks can then realize better than average returns from the sale of securities. And this is in fact what happened during these two years.

Returns to total member bank assets over the eleven year period are summarized in Table 10.7. According to our simple test for runs a strong upward trend exists in total earn-

---

[3] W. Allen Wallis and Harry V. Roberts, *Statistics: A New Approach* (Glencoe: Free Press, 1956) pp. 572-575.

[4] "The number, S, of signs of either kind will be normally distributed, in sequences of independent observation, with mean and standard deviation

$$M_s = n-1, \qquad \sigma_s = \sqrt{\frac{n+1}{12}}$$

where . . . n is the number of observations, or one more than the number of signs . . . A two-tail probability is ordinarily appropriate here . . . Letting S represent the number of plus or minus signs, whichever is less numerous, the standard normal variable, incorporating a continuity adjustment is

$$K = \frac{n-s}{\sqrt{\frac{n+1}{3}}}."$$

Ibid., pp. 273-274.

ings on member bank assets. The value of K is 4.5 which is significant at the .05 level. The same, however, is not true for net earnings before and after taxes. In both instances K=1.5 which is not significant at the .05 level.

Table 10.7

Average Percentage Distribution of Earnings on Total Assets by Year from 1950-1960 for Federal Reserve Districts 2-11 and Bank Sizes 1-5

| Year | Percentage of Total Assets | | |
	Total Earnings	Net Current Earnings Before Income Taxes	Net Profits After Taxes
1950	2.82	1.39	0.71
1951	288	1.07	0.68
1952	2.98	1.10	0.65
1953	3.10	1.12	0.63
1954	3.15	1.09	0.72
1955	3.30	1.15	0.63
1956	3.53	1.21	0.63
1957	3.70	1.19	0.65
1958	3.79	1.11	0.73
1959	4.02	1.25	0.65
1960	4.32	1.30	0.80

For the recession years 1954 and 1958 total earnings on assets did not decline nor did returns after taxes. Net current earnings before taxes, however, declined in both years. This is a pattern similar to that suggested for net current earnings before income taxes on bank capital.

To judge from the evidence and analysis presented in Chapter 9 there is a strong upward drift in returns on loans and securities during the period.

V. CONCLUSION

The evidence presented in this chapter is consistent with our hypothesis. Member banking tends to be relatively more profitable in the underdeveloped Districts. This is true whether such profitability is measured by returns on bank capital, returns on total assets or returns on loans and securities.

Returns by bank size are mixed. This is not surprising since the three measures of bank profitability provide insights into bank operations.

Dividend policy is apparently more liberal in Districts which are underdeveloped. Banks in these Districts appear to be more closely tied to the capital funds market than casual observation would suggest. This is as it should be if the capital funds market is to be useful in allocating resources.

CHAPTER 11

MEMBER BANK PORTFOLIOS: LOANS AND INVESTMENTS

I. HYPOTHESIS

If member banks are influenced by the local environment in which they operate, we should expect to observe that the composition of their portfolios is related to the degree of District economic development as that development is summarized by per capita personal income.

The purpose of this chapter is to examine the empirical consistency of this hypothesis. The analysis will attempt to ascertain if in fact portfolio holdings of loans and investments are related to (1) earnings and (2) District per capita incomes. For this purpose we shall draw on the evidence summarized in the preceding chapters particularly 8 and 9. Section II examines the relation between member bank holdings of loans and investments and earnings on such holdings. Section III analyzes the relation between loans and investments and per capita District incomes. Section IV presents the conclusion.

II. COMPOSITION OF MEMBER BANK PORTFOLIOS AND EARNINGS ON LOANS AND INVESTMENTS

One would expect higher earnings on loans to induce member banks to hold a higher percentage of their assets in the form of loans. All other things equal, in Districts where such rates prevail, banks would be expected to favor loans over investments and cash holdings.

To judge from the evidence presented in Table 8.4 and Table 9.3 the relationship between earnings and loans is not clear cut. Indeed, the evidence, such as it is, suggests the opposite relationship that returns on loans and bank holdings of loans vary inversely. The higher the returns on loans the lower the percentage of assets held in the form of loans. Thus, a rank correlation coefficient of —.163 exists. It is not, however, a particularly strong relationship since the correlation coefficient is not significant. As between Districts apparently all other things are not equal. This is not surprising. The Districts vary in their economic composition. The more industrialized ones offer more scope for making the type of loans considered "prudent" by most bankers including bank examiners even though earnings on such loans may be lower.

Perhaps more important are some implications of these and subsequent results. One implication is that member banks which we would expect to be more enlightened and sophisticated remain victims of the type of defunct ideas discussed in Chapter 3. Another implication is that the type of liquidity preference discussed in Chapter 8 is not a "Southern tradition" *per se*. On the contrary it appears throughout the banking industry.

Consider, for example, the percentage of bank holdings of assets in the form of cash. To judge from a rank correlation of +.901 which is significant at the .01 level a direct and strong relationship exists between earnings on loans and percentage of bank assets held in cash. Under the circumstances it is not surprising that a strong inverse relationship exists between the percentage holdings of government securities and earnings on loans. Thus the rank correlation coefficient is —.715 which is significant at the .05 level. When returns on loans are relatively high there is apparently a decided preference on the part of member banks to hold on to cash. By itself this is a rather surprising result.

If taken seriously this preference for cash assets would seem to suggest that member banks immobilize rather than mobilize a community's resources. To be sure all of this may be done as a consequence of "prudent" banking practices. But these practices themselves are interwoven with defunct ideas in need of searching analysis. Undoubtedly the various regulatory and supervisory agencies share in the perpetuation of ideas which make "liquidity preference" attractive to bankers. After all, an individual banker has little choice but to follow the rules of the game if he is to stay out of ruin and possibly jail. His attitude of playing it safe is understandable. Equally important on this score may be the reluctance of bankers to hold securities in the light of events in the 1950's when security losses substantially exceeded profits on securities sold and redeemed. The notable exception to such losses occurred in 1954 and 1958 when banks realized substantial gains in their securities dealings.

III.   BANK PORTFOLIO COMPOSITION AND DISTRICT PER CAPITA INCOME

We should expect to observe that in the more developed Districts a greater proportion of bank assets would be in the form of loans than in the less developed Districts. The character of the economic environment would thus tend to effect a bank's loan market. And one principal reason for such an effect is that loan markets tend to be local affairs.

In a more developed District wider scope is available for making the type of loans a banker and his overseers consider "prudent". In this sense, banks appear to play a very passive role in promoting the economic development of their localities. The old saying that "you can get a bank loan only if you don't need money" — may perhaps have application in the poorer Districts.

To judge from a rank correlation coefficient of $+.388$ a direct relationship does exist between per capita District income and the proportion of bank assets held in the form of loans. The relationship, however, is not a significant one — at least the coefficient is not statistically so since the coefficient is not significant at the .01 or .05 level. Such as it is, the evidence suggests that the asset distribution of member banks is molded by their economic environment.

Thus, for example, there is a tendency for the proportion of cash assets-held by member banks to vary inversely with per capita personal income in the District. The rank correlation coefficient for such a relationship is $-.583$. The relationship is a strong one since the coefficient is statistically signficant at the .05 level.

The proportion of government securities that member banks hold apparently varies directly with the per capita income. Thus the rank correlation coefficient is $+.328$ which is, however, not statistically significant at either the .01 or .05 levels. The evidence does suggest that banks in the more developed regions act, as a vehicle for the transfer of resources out of their Districts in the form of government securities.

Insofar as the holdings of "other securities" are concerned a direct and strong relationship exists between such holdings and income. In this instance, the rank correlation coefficient is $+.720$ and significant at the .05 level. Real estate loan holdings and District income are, apparently, inversely related as judged by a rank correlation coefficient of $-.198$ which is not, however, significant at either the .01 or .05 levels.

IV. CONCLUSION

It would appear that, on balance, member banks in the less developed Districts hold a considerable proportion of their assets in the form of cash and real estate loans. They do not apparently resort to holdings of government securities nor indeed "other securities" to the extent that member banks do in the more developed Districts. The form in which member banks hold their assets in the less developed Districts simply immobilize resources. This does not mean that in the less developed Districts bankers *per se* are not interested in pecuniary returns. It could be that the organization, structure and the rules under which member banks operate are inappropriate for the tasks at hand in the poorer Districts.

Chapter 12

INCOME AND EXPENSES OF MEMBER BANKS

I. Hypotheses

We should expect to observe that income of member banks is inversely related to the degree of District economic development. Thus banks located in the relatively under-developed Districts would be expected to have higher incomes and expenses as a per cent of their total earnings. This is because the bulk of bank income is derived from loans. And, as already discussed, higher rates on loans are realized in the more underdeveloped Districts. If, as some argue, bank expenses tend to be fixed, or at least mainly so, we should not expect such expenses to vary with the degree of District economic development.

We should also expect to observe that expenses do not vary with the size of banks.[1] The fact of almost constant costs as the size of bank increases is suggested by David Alhadeff and which he agrees is characteristic of the banking industry. The purpose of this chapter is to examine the empirical consistency of these hypotheses. Section II examines the experience of member banks in the 2-11 Federal Reserve Districts. Section III considers income and expenses by bank size. Section IV examines member bank experience over the period 1950-60. Section V presents the conclusions.

II. Experience of Member Banks in Districts 2-11

To judge from the evidence summarized in Table 12.1, and in the order of their importance, the sources of bank earnings as a percentage of total earnings are interest on loans, interest on U.S. Government securities, service charges, interest and dividends on "other securities," and "other current earnings."

This is about what we would expect since the principal occupation of commercial banks is in the field of loans and

---

[1] David A. Alhadeff, *Monopoly and Competition in Banking* (Berkeley: University of California Press, 1954) pp. 84 ff.

Table 12.1

Average Percentage Distribution of Sources and Disposition of Earnings by Federal Reserve Districts for Years 1950-1960 and Bank Sizes 1-5

Federal Reserve District	Sources and Disposition of Earnings (% of Total Earnings)					
	Interest on U.S. Gov't Securities	Interest and Dividends on Other Securities	Earnings on Loans	Other Current Earnings	Service Charges on Deposit Accounts	Salaries and Wages
2	23.44	7.02	57.33	5.04	7.16	29.97
3	25.40	7.15	58.82	8.63	4.01	26.11
4	26.32	6.17	57.65	9.85	4.97	26.82
5	22.94	5.15	61.85	5.29	4.77	27.97
6	21.92	6.26	59.01	5.99	6.82	30.74
7	29.94	5.64	52.76	5.45	6.20	30.70
8	28.46	6.37	55.91	9.25	4.63	30.50
9	24.94	6.01	53.44	15.61	6.57	30.13
10	23.99	5.42	58.33	12.26	7.44	33.87
11	20.64	6.15	62.18	11.02	6.28	34.53

Table 12.1 (continued)

Sources and Disposition of Earnings (% of Total Earnings)

Federal Reserve District	Interest on Time Deposits	Other Current Expenses	Total Expenses	Net Current Earnings Before Income Taxes	Net Losses or Profits	Taxes on Net Income	Net Profits
2	18.12	22.56	70.64	29.36	-3.06	7.67	17.36
3	18.80	21.93	66.84	33.16	-2.97	8.66	20.47
4	16.06	22.92	65.81	34.19	-2.77	9.34	20.85
5	16.13	21.58	65.68	34.32	-2.13	10.58	20.54
6	10.58	36.09	66.83	33.17	-2.96	9.25	19.46
7	14.10	21.52	66.30	33.68	-2.59	8.88	20.55
8	9.91	22.85	63.26	36.90	-3.53	9.59	22.74
9	15.39	21.20	66.72	33.28	-2.83	9.64	19.71
10	7.43	21.32	62.62	37.38	-3.76	10.17	22.47
11	4.90	24.87	64.30	35.70	-5.30	8.65	20.58

investments. Banks in Districts 5, 6 and 11 appear to do somewhat better as a percentage of total earnings derived from interest on loans than banks elsewhere. They also derive less from interest on U. S. Government securities than banks located in other Districts. Banks in Districts 2 and 10 lead other banks in the earnings that they derive from service charges on deposit accounts. The most favorable on this score are banks in District 3 whose service charges as a percentage of total earnings is the lowest.

According to our hypothesis we should expect to observe that an inverse relationship exists between bank earnings on loans as a percentage of total earnings and the degree of economic development in the District. The rank correlation coefficient for such a relationship is —.369. Thus the evidence is consistent with the hypothesis. The relationship, however, is not strong since the coefficient is not statistically significant at either the .01 or .05 levels.

We should expect to observe that banks in the more developed Districts derive more of their income as a percentage of total earnings in interest from U.S. Government securities than banks located in the less developed Districts. Thus the evidence should be consistent with a direct relationship between these two variables. And, in fact, the rank correlation coefficient is +.388 suggesting that a positive relationship does exist between earnings derived from U.S. Government securities and degree of District development. Although the sign of the coefficient is correct, the coefficient itself is not statistically significant at either the .01 or .05 levels. This suggests that although a relationship in the expected direction does exist it is not strong.

A similar situation would be expected to exist in the case of earnings from "other securities." The relationship, however, is much weaker. A rank correlation coefficient of +.118 suggests that the relationship is positive as expected. It is not a very strong relation as indicated by the fact that the coefficient is not statistically significant at either the .01 or .05 levels. Banks in some of the relatively underdeveloped Districts, apparently, also derive a substantial fraction of their total earnings from interest on other securities.

Since the 1930's service charges have been in use as a

means for supplementing a bank's income. At the same time, such charges are also used to discourage unprofitable accounts and encourage the maintenance of larger balances. This is a "luxury" that banks located in the more developed and wealthier Districts can afford. Banks not so located can ill afford to discourage deposits by such means. We should accordingly expect to observe that service charges and the extent of District economic development to be directly related. A rank correlation coefficient of +.136 does suggest that service charges and District development are in fact directly related. But the coefficient's lack of statistical significance at either the .01 or .05 levels suggests that service charges are a sufficiently widespread banking practice and only weakly related to the degree of District economic development. The evidence does suggest, however, that banks in the more developed Districts apparently tend to resort more to such charges than banks located elsewhere.

Member bank expenses as a percentage of total earnings summarized in Table 12.1 indicate that the principal expense item are salaries and wages. Banks located in District 11 outpace their counterparts elsewhere in wages and salaries as a percentage of total earnings. These expenses may be cut through automation and other devices. And banks undoubtedly do resort to these devices to cut expenses. This is particularly true for the routine operations in a bank. Banks located in the less developed Districts may not be under the same pressure to automate routine work because the wages of personnel engaged in such work may be lower than in the more developed District.

It is however another matter when the issue concerns bank officers and other senior officials. Demand for their talents is probably considerably greater than for routine office workers. And if banks are to remain of service to the economy the quality of their top personnel must be maintained if indeed, in some instances, not improved.

All of this suggests that we should expect to observe that an inverse relationship exists between wages and salaries as a percentage of total bank earnings and the degree of District economic development. This relation is suggested by a rank correlation coefficient —.393, although it is not statistically significant at either the .01 or .05 levels.

The other singularly important expense item to banks is interest on time deposits. This problem tends to be "solved" for banks by various regulations and regulatory agencies. Limits are placed on rates banks are permitted to pay their depositors. Nonetheless, banks are well advised to pay for their principal inputs what they are worth to them. They should endeavor, in effect, to attract as many deposits as they can profitably employ. In view of the explicit and implicit regulations governing the types of loans that member banks are permitted to make, banks in the more developed Districts have greater opportunity to make the type of loans considered "prudent." In addition, the more developed Districts would also tend to generate a greater volume of bank deposits.

Accordingly, we should expect to observe that a positive relationship exists between interest on time deposits as a percentage of total earnings, and the degree of District development. To judge from a rank correlation coefficient of +.496 the evidence is consistent with the hypothesis. The coefficient, however, is not statistically significant at either the .01 or .05 levels suggesting that the relationship is not very strong.

The foregoing evidence and analysis suggests that total bank expenses are positively related to District development. And, in fact, this is the conclusion one reaches on the basis of a rank correlation coefficient of +.424 between total bank expenses and the degree of District development. The coefficient, however, is not statistically significant at either the .01 or .05 levels.

Even within the severe restrictions imposed on lending, banking in the relatively underdeveloped Districts would tend to be somewhat riskier than elsewhere. Available evidence summarized in a rank correlation coefficient of —.105 between losses to banks and District development suggests that a relationship in the expected directions exists. Losses to banks are universally related to District development. But other factors apparently are also important. For example, the losses on securities which have been widespread throughout the banking system for the bulk of the period under consideration have probably reduced the significance of the above relationship.

Taxes on net income and net profits as a percentage of total earnings are related inversely to the degree of District development. These relations are suggested by rank correlation coefficients of —.405 between taxes on net income and District development and —.177 between net profits and District development. The results are about what we would expect even though neither of the coefficients is statistically significant at either the .01 or .05 levels.

III. EARNINGS AND EXPENSES BY BANK SIZE

To judge from data summarized in Table 12.2 a clear-cut trend in earnings and expenses by bank size does not exist. As a percentage of total earnings, earnings on loans decline with bank size. "Other current" earnings, on the other hand, increase as do service charges on deposits and interest and dividends on "other securities." But even in these cases the pattern is not uniform. As a source of earnings, for example, service charges on deposits increase as we move from the smaller to the larger banks but decrease when we reach the largest bank even though in such banks this source of earnings is more important than in the smallest bank.

According to Alhadeff's argument, the banking industry very nearly represents a constant cost operation. The evidence summarized in the above table suggests that his argument is not without some support. Indeed the comparative stability of the item "total expenses" lends fairly strong support to Alhadeff's argument. It should be noted, however, that costs discussed in traditional theory and the expense items displayed above are not strictly comparable and the latter items are intended only to be suggestive and not technically precise.[2]

IV. EXPERIENCE IN THE PERIOD 1950-60.

The evidence summarized in Table 12.3 suggests a downward drift in the percentage of total earnings derived from

---

[2] See also Alhadeff's discussion of this same point *ibid.*, p. 83.

Table 12.2

Average Percentage Distribution of Sources and Disposition of Earnings by Bank Size for Federal Reserve Districts 2-11* and for Years 1950-1960

	Size I	Size II	Size III	Size IV	Size V
Percentage of Total Earnings:					
Interest on U.S. Gov't. securities	24.94	26.07	25.09	24.96	24.00
Interest and Dividends on other securities	4.98	6.21	6.97	6.44	5.68
Earnings on loans	60.35	57.70	56.35	55.55	55.36
Other current earnings	8.17	7.89	9.11	9.94	11.94
Service charges on deposit accounts	5.21	5.60	6.48	6.71	6.01
Salaries and wages	32.54	30.18	29.21	29.23	29.07
Interest on time deposits	10.90	13.24	14.18	14.17	11.58
Other current expenses	22.55	22.52	23.41	24.46	24.66
Total expenses	65.67	65.39	65.89	66.58	64.37
Net current earnings before income taxes	34.33	34.62	34.10	33.42	36.96
Net losses or profits	-3.02	-3.28	-3.70	-2.80	-2.51
Taxes on net income	7.73	8.66	9.65	10.59	13.31
Net Profits	22.99	21.68	19.28	18.01	18.65

*Owing to the lack of comparable data on earnings and expenses, sizes IV and V exclude District 2 for all years and district 7 for the years 1950-51.

interest on U.S. Government securities. Our simple test of runs yields a K of 3.5 which is significant at the .05 level and suggests a significant downward trend. This is not true for earnings derived from other securities. In fact, a K of 1.5 is obtained in this category indicating neither a significant upward nor downward movement in the series.

As we would expect a significant upward movement is indicated in earnings on loans. Our simple test yields a K of 4.5 which is significant at the .05 level. A significant upward trend is also indicated in the series "other current earnings." In this instance K=5.5 which is significant at the .05 level. Service charges, on the other hand, do not reveal a significant movement in either direction as indicated by K=1.5 which is not significant at the .05 level.

When expenses are considered, the only item in which a significant movement is detected by our test is the upward trend in "interest on time deposits." The value of K 4.5 which is significant at the .05 level. No significant trend is detected in "total expenses." Apparently banks reduced other expense items sufficiently to accommodate the upward movements in interest payments on time deposits without at the same time increasing total bank expenses. Thus, for example, the items salaries and wages and "other current expenses" are somewhat reduced.

Cyclically, three items tend to stand above the others. In the recession years of 1954 and 1958 an upward spurt occurred in the item "total expenses." The item "net losses or profits" turned into profits in both years. And the reason for such a turn is discussed in preceding chapters. Moreover the series on net profits suggest the stability in profits one would expect in the banking business.

V. CONCLUSION

The evidence and analyses summarized in this chapter suggest that the principal source of member bank earnings is derived from loans. Banks located in the less developed Districts derive a somewhat higher percentage of their total earnings from loans than banks located in the more developed Districts. Although the evidence tends to support the several

Table 12.3

Average Percentage Distribution of Sources and Disposition of Earnings by Year
from 1950-1960 for Federal Reserve Districts 2-11 and Bank Sizes 1-5

	Sources and Disposition of Earnings (% of Total Earnings)					
Year	Interest on U.S. Gov't. Securities	Interest and Dividends on Other Securities	Earnings on Loans	Other Current Earnings	Service Charges on Deposit Accounts	Salaries and Wages
1950	27.74	5.79	53.65	10.10	6.26	30.10
1951	25.87	5.79	55.86	9.78	6.18	30.87
1952	25.82	5.74	56.71	9.16	5.83	30.69
1953	26.29	5.64	56.75	8.76	5.71	31.01
1954	25.50	5.84	57.22	8.85	5.91	31.33
1955	24.82	5.79	58.22	8.62	5.86	31.05
1956	24.95	5.84	58.32	8.34	5.85	30.76
1957	24.82	6.08	58.34	8.22	5.93	30.31
1958	23.23	7.02	58.88	8.21	6.10	30.28
1959	23.93	6.81	58.83	7.88	5.92	28.72
1960	23.74	6.83	59.23	7.66	5.93	28.08

Table 12.3 (continued)

Sources and Disposition of Earnings (% of Total Earnings)

Year	Interest on Time Deposits	Other Current Expenses	Total Expenses	Net Current Earnings Before Income Taxes	Net Losses or Profits	Taxes on Net Income	Net Profits
1950	9.39	23.22	62.70	37.30	−3.68	8.29	25.33
1951	9.20	22.96	63.03	36.97	−4.40	8.96	23.61
1952	9.67	22.58	62.93	37.07	−3.67	10.46	22.21
1953	10.77	22.73	63.88	36.12	−4.04	10.78	20.67
1954	11.61	23.05	65.37	34.63	+0.84	10.98	23.10
1955	11.63	22.92	64.93	35.07	−3.71	10.27	19.15
1956	12.51	22.89	65.41	34.59	−5.46	8.67	18.16
1957	15.28	23.22	67.74	32.26	−3.95	8.38	17.94
1958	17.57	23.90	70.49	29.51	+1.42	8.98	19.64
1959	17.88	23.53	68.88	31.10	−5.86	7.50	16.44
1960	19.47	23.49	69.77	30.22	−2.25	7.60	18.73

hypotheses discussed, the support is not very strong. This would suggest that banks in the several Districts are under the influence of factors which transcend the degree of District economic development.

Over time the downward drift in the percentage of earnings obtained from U.S. Government securities and the upward drift in loans is confirmed by the evidence. This is perhaps the most significant event in post-war banking for it represents a return to the principal function of banking which is the production of loans and not simply the financing of government.

By bank size an evidence tends to confirm the argument that banking is very nearly a constant cost industry. This should be immediately qualified by the observation that the evidence is only suggestive and not definitive since neither the costs of traditional theory nor those typically used in the analysis, say, of a manufacturing plant are used.

CHAPTER 13

MEMBER BANK CAPITAL

I. Hypotheses

Professor J. B. McFerrin suggested in 1947 that the capital position of southern banking left much to be desired. In effect, the capital position at the time was inadequate. By the late 1950's, however, the evidence summarized in Chapter 5 suggests that the capital position of southern banks as on par with banks elsewhere in the country.

The purpose of this chapter is to examine the extent to which the capital position of member banks is related to District economic development. Accordingly a tentative hypothesis is advanced that we should expect to observe that the capital "strength" of these banks is directly related to the degree of District economic development. Accordingly a tentative hypothesis is advanced that we should expect to observe that the capital "strength" of these banks is directly related to the degree of District development. The more developed the District the "stronger" the capital position of banks.[1] In addition, we should also expect to observe that the capital position of banks varies universally with bank size.[2] Section II discusses the special nature of bank capital. Section III examines the empirical consistency of the hypothesis against member bank data for Districts 2-11. Section IV considers the experience of member banks by deposit size. Section V presents the capital position of member banks over the period 1950-60. Section VI presents the conclusion.

II. Special Nature of Bank Capital

The principal function of capital in commercial banking is unlike that in other industries. In such industries as manufacturing and utilities, for example, capital provides funds

---

[1] David A. Alhadeff, *Monopoly and Competition in Banking* (Berkeley: University of California Press, 1954) p. 189.
[2] *Ibid.*, p. 189.

for acquiring the tangible means for conducting business. Although this is also true in commercial banking in the sense that capital provides funds for buildings and equipment, its principal function is to serve as a guarantee of funds.[3]

Some idea of the functions of bank capital is obtained from data furnished by the Federal Deposit Insurance Corporation for all commercial banks. On December 31, 1959, for example, capital funds amounted to about $19 billion while investment in buildings and equipment amounted to only about $2.5 billion. Since the bulk of funds are held in highly liquid forms such as government securities, a considerable amount of a community's resources are in effect immobilized.

Bank capital provides a cushion to absorb possible losses so that depositors will receive some protection and assures the public, including business enterprise, of a bank's ability to meet its obligations promptly even under conditions which result in losses on its principal products which are loans and investments. It is also used to satisfy requirements of supervisory authorities regarding the adequacy of capital in relation to risks in carrying out the business of commercial banking.

Primary sources of capital employed in commercial banking are the same as for other industries. They are retained earnings and the issue of stock. And as in other industries these two sources are dependent in no small degree on the rates of return, or profit, that capital realizes in the undertaking.

In the period since the war, however, the source of capital derived from the issuance of proprietary rights in banking has dwindled to the extent that increases in bank capital from this source account for only 18 per cent while that from retained earnings account for 82 per cent.[4] This proportion stands in marked contrast, for example, to the utilities industry which has managed to obtain the bulk of its new capital through the market by issuance of new equities.

---

[3] American Bankers Association, *The Commercial Banking Industry* (Englewood-Cliffs, N.J.: Prentice-Hall, Inc., 1962) p. 332.
[4] *Ibid.*, p. 325.

Commercial banking's heavy dependence on retained earnings as a source of new capital is understandable. When other industries turn to the market for new capital they do so with the expectation that the new acquisitions will increase earning power sufficiently to cover the cost. Banks, however, are usually not so fortunate. Additional capital can increase a bank's earning ability if it has a favorable effect on liberalizing its lending and investing policy.[5] The increase in earnings which may result, however, would have to be balanced against the risk costs incurred which may be significant enough to swamp any increase in returns. Another way in which increased capital could increase a bank's earning power is if it attracted more deposits. Little evidence exists, however, that such in fact is the case.[6] Under these circumstances the issuance of new bank equities may adversely affect on balance existing stockholders by decreasing per-share profits.

This tendency on the part of the commercial banking industry to dip into earnings as a means for raising new capital funds rather than going to the market for such funds raises a problem for the economy as a whole.[7] What is to prevent banks, for example, from creating "excess capacity" in the sense of excess liquidity in the commercial banking industry? Surely not the market. The connection between the market and the banking industry, insofar as new capital funds are concerned, is very loose.

Little relief to the problem can be expected from our tax laws. By discriminating between wealth and income, the tax system ironically reinforces the already existing tendency toward excess capacity in commercial banking. And it does so in the following way. A significant number of the country's banks are dominated by closely knit groups or indeed families holding a sizeable proportion of capital stock.[8] These people tend to view the question of retained earnings quite differently from a larger and more heterogeneous group of investors. This is understandable. They are after all, justified in taking into

[5] Ronald I. Robinson, *The Management of Bank Funds* (New York: Mc-Graw-Hill, 1962) p. 434.
[6] *Ibid.*, p. 435.
[7] I am indebted to my colleague Professor Zarko G. Bilbija for several observations in this and the following paragraph.
[8] Robinson, *op cit.*, pp. 437-438.

account how the distribution or retention of earnings will affect their taxes. And since tax laws tend to favor the retention of earnings who can blame a closely knit group from plowing these earnings back into the business even if it is not always certain that it is in society's best interest to do so. Even more important, perhaps, is the fact that government regulatory agencies encourage increases in bank capital and in the interests of "sound banking." Pressures stemming from self interest *and* government working in the same direction are not likely to go unheeded by many people.

All of this, of course, does not mean that capital requirements in banking should be abandoned. For reasons already stated quite the contrary is true. A wider and more heterogeneous ownership of bank stock, however, should be encouraged as a means for tightening up the links between commercial banking and the capital funds market. Directors of banks would then of necessity take more of a trustee attitude when confronted with a bank's capital needs and the problem of dividend distribution. On this score the post-war trends are encouraging. An increasing number of banks now have thousands of share holders. For this reason the returns to capital in banking are assuming an increasing importance in obtaining additional capital funds and indeed in maintaining existing capital within the banking industry.

III. CAPITAL POSITION OF MEMBER BANKS BY DISTRICT

Three measures are useful in gauging the capital strength of banks. One is the ratio of capital funds to total deposits. This is the most direct measure indicating, in a sense, the ability of a bank to protect its depositors. The second measure which is the ratio of capital funds to assets is at times preferable in that losses are incurred not on liabilities but on assets. The third measure is the ratio of capital to "risk assets." This measure is at times more useful than the second because it recognizes differences in risk among assets. It is constructed by considering all assets other than cash and U. S. Government securities as "risk assets." In the remainder of this chapter all three measures will be considered.

Table 13.1

Average Percentage Distribution of Capital Ratios by Federal Reserve Districts for Years 1950-60 and Bank Sizes 1-5

Federal Reserve Districts

Capital Ratios:	2	3	4	5	6	7	8	9	10	11
Total capital accounts to:										
Total Assets	8.52	10.17	8.76	8.61	7.74	7.14	8.05	7.33	8.16	8.06
Total Assets — Gov't Securities and Cash Assets	19.02	23.19	21.36	20.22	18.79	19.68	22.55	18.13	21.35	20.53
Total Deposits	9.49	11.47	9.71	9.58	8.54	7.79	8.89	8.00	9.01	8.80

According to our hypothesis, we should expect to observe that the capital strength of member banks is directly related to the degree of District development. To judge from the evidence summarized in Table 13.1 and a rank correlation coefficient of $+.316$ between the ratio of total capital accounts to deposits the relationship is in the direction expected by our hypothesis. Conclusions derived from this measure of capital strength are confirmed by the other two measures. Thus the rank correlation coefficient between the ratio of capital to total assets and District income is $+.340$. As for the ratio of capital to "risk assets" and District income the relationship yields a rank correlation coefficient of $+.360$. Although the correlation coefficients for all three measures are of the "correct" sign suggesting that our hypothesis is consistent with the evidence, the relationship between member bank capital strength and degree of District development is not statistically significant at either the .01 or .05 levels.

Such as it is, the evidence suggests that the capital position of member banks in the less developed Districts tends to be weaker than that of banks located in the more developed Districts. If we take the pronouncements of bankers seriously that a function of bank capital is to insure the ability to acquire risk assets, member banks in the poorer Districts are not as well equipped to acquire such assets as banks elsewhere. This inadequacy is reinforced by greater risks incurred in the less developed Districts.

In view of the greater returns to bank capital in these Districts we should expect all other things equal, that more bank capital will ultimately be attracted to the poorer Districts. And we may very well be witnessing just such a movement of resources. The barriers to such a movement in the form of various states and federal restrictions on banking are not trivial. Bankers may in fact have a legitimate complaint when they argue that the returns to bank capital are "inadequate." They may very well be "inadequate" to attract capital in face of various restrictions imposed on banking.

IV. CAPITAL "STRENGTH" BY BANK SIZE

To judge from the evidence summarized in Table 13.2 bank capital "strength" does vary inversely with bank size. All three measures of such "strength" decline as the size of bank increases.

Table 13.2

Average Percentage Distribution of Capital Ratios by Bank Size for Federal Reserve Districts 2-11 and for Years 1950-1960

	Size I	Size II	Size III	Size IV	Size V
Capital Ratios:					
Total Capital Accounts to:					
Total Assets	9.76	8.41	7.62	7.18	6.73
Total Assets Less Gov't Securities and cash assets	25.70	21.39	18.31	17.01	16.02
Total Deposits	10.91	9.27	8.36	7.88	7.32

This is about what we would expect and the results are consistent with Alhadeff's findings.[9] Thus, for example, the inverse relation between the ratio of capital to deposits and bank size can be attributed to the gravitation of deposits to larger banks owing to their prestige, urban location and to the fact that such banks often act as correspondents for rural banks. Moreover, the larger banks can also afford to be less liquid than smaller organizations and so the existence of an inverse relation between the ratio of capital to "risk assets" and bank size. The lower ratio of capital to total assets in the larger banks seems to suggest the greater confidence against losses that prevail in these banks.

---

[9] Alhadeff, op. cit., p. 189.

V. MEMBER BANK CAPITAL: 1950-60

To judge from the evidence summarized in Table 13.3 and our simple test for runs the overall capital position of member banks is improving. Thus, significant upward trends are detected in the ratio of capital to total assets and in the ratio of capital to total deposits. For the first $K=3.5$ and for the second $K=4.5$ and both are statistically significant at the .05 level.

The so-called capital to "risk assets" ratio declined throughout most of the period. In view of the greater earning rates obtained by banks on loans it is little wonder that they have ventured into riskier fields than simply cash and government securities. The unpegging of U.S. Government securities in the earlier 1950's probably speeded up the departure of banks into other securities and loans. The net effect has been a decline in the capital to "risk assets" even though the other two measures of capital strength registered increases. If the trend continues, many regulatory agencies will be forced to seriously re-consider the thinking underlying the adequacy of bank as it is judged by the ratio of capital to "risk assets."

The capital strength of member banks over the period studied varies according to the measure with which one chooses to measure such strength. It is, for example, not at all clear that all commercial banks must of necessity raise large amounts of additional capital if they are to assure their ability to acquire risk assets.[10] Such a case could probably be made for banks located in the less developed Districts but with much less certainty for banks in the developed Districts.

VI. CONCLUSION

The evidence and analyses summarized in this chapter supports the argument that banks in the more developed Districts also tend to be in a stronger capital position. Since bank capital is presumably an important factor determining the ability of banks to undertake risks, banks located in the less

---

[10] American Bankers Association, *op. cit.*, p. 325.

Table 13.3

Average Percentage Distribution of Capital Ratios by Year from 1950-1960
for Federal Reserve Districts 2-11 and Bank Sizes 1-5

	1950	1951	1952	1953	1954	1955	1956	1957	1958	1959	1960
Other Ratios:											
Total Capital Accounts to:											
Total Assets	7.56	7.73	7.67	7.83	8.00	8.21	8.45	8.57	8.71	8.65	9.00
Total Assets Less Gov't. Securities and Cash Assets	22.92	22.15	21.44	21.13	20.74	20.36	19.87	19.95	19.32	18.69	18.58
Total Deposits	8.30	8.48	8.32	8.60	8.79	9.07	9.35	9.53	9.70	9.64	10.07

developed Districts where risks are greater are less able than banks elsewhere to undertake such risk owing to a weaker capital position.

The inverse relation between the measures of bank capital strength and the size of banks suggests that the measures themselves are imperfect. Peculiarities of bank capital suggest that capital *per se* may not be as important a factor in gauging the strength of a bank as it is in, say, a manufacturing plant.

Over the period of this study two measures of bank capital strength have been increasing significantly. Thus the capital to deposit ratio and the capital to total assets ratio have registered significant upward trend during the period 1950-60. The decline of the ratio of capital to risk assets is largely the consequences of the unpegging of the U.S. Government securities market and as a result the decrease in holding of U.S. Government securities on the part of banks. In addition the relatively stable economic conditions in the 1950's bolstered the courage of many a banker to venture into "risker" fields.

CHAPTER 14

IN RETROSPECT

The evidence and analyses presented in this study suggests that the three part hypothesis advanced by Professor T. W. Schultz is useful in gaining insight into commercial banking in the several Federal Reserve Districts.

The poorer Federal Reserve Districts are on the peripheries of economic development in the United States. Consisting of the 5th, 6th, 10th and 11th Districts, they form a crescent shaped area of relative economic underdevelopment which is primarily rural rather than industrial-urban. The rates of return to member banks are higher in these Districts than they are elsewhere. And this is true whether the measure considered is rates of return on bank loans, bank assets, or bank capital.

Experience within a single District, in this case the 6th Federal Reserve District, suggests that significant variation in rates of return on member bank loans between centers and peripheries of development does not exist. It may be that the hypothesis is insensitive to intra-District variations owing to the compact nature of the District. In may also be, as already suggested, the consequence of excluding from the tests the very poor counties. These counties are excluded because adequate data are not available. The reason for this is the lack of member banks in the poor counties and because of the desire on the part of individual bankers to keep their operations confidential — a desire which Federal Reserve Banks tend to respect. For example, the staff of the Federal Reserve Bank of Atlanta collected and classified earnings ratios of member banks employed in Chapter 7 by bank size and location.

The "Southern Tradition" hypothesis advanced by Professor Nicholls to explain Southern underdevelopment is not entirely satisfactory. Similar conditions of underdevelopment exist in other Federal Reserve Districts which are not in the grips of a "Southern Tradition." Moreover, if the South is defined so as to include the 5th and 6th Federal Reserve Districts, the performance of their member banks in such critical areas as the loan market tends to be slightly better than member banks in the other Districts.

Much the same can be said for an implication of Professor Dunn's hypothesis for commercial banking. Other areas than the South are under the influence of an "adverse" business mix. Such an influence does not prevent member banks in these areas, including also the South, from obtaining relatively better rates of return on their loans, assets, and capital than banks servicing areas with a "favorable" business mix.

The hypotheses advanced by Professors Clark, McDonald and Ratchford are useful in the sense that the implications for commercial banking are similar to those derived from Professor T. W. Schultz's hypothesis. Returns to member banks are in fact inversely associated with the degree of economic development. Better rates of return are realized by banks on the peripheries of economic development.

In view of the passive role that the above hypotheses assign to monetary and banking phenomena, they leave something to be desired in promoting our understanding of the processes of economic development. This study advances the hypothesis, not entirely novel, that monetary and banking forces have helped to create in the relatively underdeveloped Federal Reserve Districts an atmosphere favorable to economic stagnation. The historical evidence on the influence of these forces in such regions as the South is consistent with the "monetary hypothesis."

Significant advances have been made since the monetary and banking reforms of the 1930's. Unfortunately, the commercial banking system as it is reflected in member bank operations in the decade 1950-60 does not seem to be contributing as much as it probably could in promoting regional economic development. Thus, the evidence indicates that, characteristically, member banks in the less developed Districts in spite of the higher rates of returns on loans, hold a considerable proportion of their assets in cash and real estate loans.[1] These banks do not resort to holdings of government securities or "other securities" to the extent that member banks do in the more developed Districts. The net effect would seem to be that the form in which member banks hold their assets in the underdeveloped Districts simply immobilizes needed resources for local development.

This does not mean that bankers *per se* are responsible for conditions in the less developed Districts. It could be that the organization, structure, and rules under which member banks operate are inappropriate for the tasks at hand in the poorer Districts. Many of the laws governing state and national banking are, for example, antiquated and based largely on defunct ideas and all too frequently so is their interpretation by state and federal authorities. On the other hand, some bankers have benefited, in the sense for example, that archaic laws against branch banking often preserve "pockets of monopoly."

Various attempts have been made to free American Commercial banking from the mold of the 1930's in which it was cast by the banking reforms of that period. These attempts have met with varying degrees of success. Currency Comptroller James Saxon's suggestions that if national banks are impowered to open more branches irrespective of state law, not only will national banking be strengthened but also bank competition will be increased and "local monopolies" reduced.[2] This suggestion has prompted worries elsewhere about too much concentration in banking.

Another effort by Mr. Saxon to strengthen national banking is to permit wider scope for investment dealings by national banks and state-chartered Federal Reserve Sys-

---

[1] Efforts to fill the gap in the loan market in underdeveloped areas on the part of such organizations as the Small Business Administration have not been singularly successful. There is, for example, a substantial difference between interest rates paid by firms on SBA loans which tends to be in favor of the more developed areas. "In Pennsylvania 67 direct loans were made at 4 per cent and only 6 at 5.5 per cent during the last half of 1961 . . . Georgia, South Carolina, and Arkansas tend strongly to pay the higher rate . . ." Marshall R. Colberg "Economics of Area Development" in George Macesich, *ed. Essays on Florida Economic Development* (Tallahassee: Council on Economic Development, 1963) p. 39.

[2] "Battling Bankers" *Wall Street Journal*, October 9, 1963.

tem members in revenue bonds issued by cities for such projects as toll bridges. The Federal Reserve System, however, argues that Mr. Saxon is wrong and that neither national nor state member banks can do this. The net effect is that banks are not sure what they can do.

Other efforts are not without their partisans. One, for example, revives "an old idea for legislation to move Mr. Saxon and his office from the Treasury to the Federal Reserve Board where the more conservative majority would be likely to keep his policies in line with theirs."[3] Taken seriously it suggests that perhaps Mr. Saxon has been too vocal in his demands for banking reform.

Representative Wright Patman, the Texas Democrat, insists on more fundamental reform.[4] According to his views the place to start is the Federal Reserve System itself. His views are in effect a revival of the historical issues discussed in Chapter 3 and never seriously resolved. Indeed, Mr. Patman argues that "any Federal institution that has not been looked into for nearly 30 years should have a check-up . . . we should look at the most powerful banking system on earth, our Federal Reserve System, in the light of the United States in 1964."[5] Considering the evidence and analyses summarized in this study such concern as expressed by Mr. Patman and others is of little surprise.

---

[3] *Ibid.*

[4] GOP Hopes to Stir Johnson Into Disavowal of Patman Bid to Curtail Federal Reserve Power." *Wall Street Journal,* January 22, 1964, and "Reserve Board Uniting Against Bid by Patman to Curb Its Autonomy", *Wall Street Journal,* January 24, 1964.
[5] "Patman Seeking Reserve Change" *New York Times,* January 20, 1964.

INDEX